T0063076

SPIRIT REVEALING

*God's truth concerning the
dead coming to life*

ELDON WARD

WESTBOW
PRESS
A DIVISION OF THOMAS NELSON
& ZONDERVAN

WestBow Press books may be ordered through booksellers or by contacting:

WestBow Press
A Division of Thomas Nelson & Zondervan
1663 Liberty Drive
Bloomington, IN 47403
www.westbowpress.com
1 (866) 928-1240

ISBN: 978-1-4908-5420-5 (sc)
ISBN: 978-1-4908-5419-9 (e)

Library of Congress Control Number: 2014917401

Printed in the United States of America.

WestBow Press rev. date: 10/14/2014

Contents

Author: Was born and raised in the mountains of southeast Oklahoma. First education came through the facts of nature. Of which, there is no deception, it is, what it is. If nature is honored and respected it will provide basic needs for a person. If not, it will bring starvation or injury unto death. It gives a sense of freedom that cannot be known by people that live in congregations.

Acquired a G.E.D. while in the army. Learned truth of man and his nature in the Nam. Not the enemy; he only wanted to kill, but none combat people. Afterwards, received a degree in business at Eastern Ok. State college. Crowning education was as most people whom actually work for a living. A PHD. in hard knocks of life. It is mainly achieved from too much spontaneous action with not nearly enough beforehand deliberation.

Since earliest memories, it was felt there had to be a power greater than man or so-called mother-nature. Though, not remembering the first time the words "God or Jesus" was heard, throughout life many people had been heard speaking their understanding or opinion.

Beginning at an early age, reading what most people call, "the Bible". The book, itself, says it is scripture or knowledge from God; through the life and times of people in past history. Many things would have been impossible to comprehend or believe, had it not been witnessed through powers of nature and the true nature of man through war.

The majority of people (in twenty-first century) whom speak about "God and Jesus", have spoken from the perspective of one that were raised in a congregational life style. To which is more from imagination than from a natural order of all things. Always reluctant to put much stock in their speaking because, as a whole, congregational living makes some people feel superior and others to feel inferior. What is the possible understanding in a person feeling they have to tell other people how to live their life? Surely, there can be no understanding a person (adult, above age of accountability) thinking they have to be lead through life!

Many have gone through life in a more easy appearance than this author. However, each person has only one chance at life, whether each does it good or poor, should they not be allowed to live it for self? United States Government sends young men around the world to die, in stating, this to be fact. Yet, in country, citizens are imprisoned for not allowing supposed-superior to live citizen's lives (away from constitution/liberty & justice for all)! Are not "God and Jesus" of the same opinion for man, as was the forefathers of the United States? For, they have ten basic laws for all men to live by. To which, there would be no need for governments, run by the opinion of those feeling superior. ECC.3:14 **I know that whatever God does endures forever; nothing can be added to it, nor anything taken from it; God has made it so, in order that men should fear before Him.**

From knowing, most whom claim to know very well "God and Jesus", but know very little actual truth about them, this author has done intense search in the scripture and history. Even this study did little more than the used-car-salesmanship that was heard from those "claiming" to have been called by God.

Then one day realizing, if there is an awesome-powered-God of all things, why would He cast His pearls before those that did not trust Him/would not believe Him? Even nature teaches enough to know He is true! Case and point, why would men even try to teach Him, where not following His word, says, they do not believe Him?

Fact: a lustful-mind can be controlled through deception in truth!

Could it be, man of political-mind, knowing, most people sense an awesome God, can control hearts & minds of other people, while not realizing their own mind is being controlled? Yet, those holding to every word out of the mouth of God, instantly see the deception!

If and when other people come to the same experience with the Spirit of God, as has this author, they will see the scripture in a much brighter light! Once a half dozen different prophecy teachings from the Spirit, have been learned, the scripture starts coming together as a whole teaching. For, this is the way of God; He is one and He is complete!

This author compiled a few findings, as they came through research and was explained by the Spirit, through the scripture. Therefore, one that has not had the same experience with God as has this author, will find it a hard read (**seal it up amongst the disciples**). However, the majority is scripture and history, with a little insert of personal feeling.

The purpose and goal in writing this book is to generate a thought process in as many people as possible. <u>Because of the fact</u>: **Many will knock but few will enter! --- The whole world wonders after the beast and worships his image!**

Preface

- *Revised Standard Version,* Thomas Nelson & Sons, 1952
- Zondervan KJV
- multiple history books, but only when two or more say the same
- Corpus Juri Canonic
- 65 years of life's teaching

CONSIDER: Do I truly believe God? Do I truly believe Jesus? Or, am I just following perceived-society? The prophets and Jesus said every word out of the mouth of God would come to pass. If Jesus is truly the son of God, then today, something has to be wrong with mainstream Christianity. Simply because, Jesus said **many will knock but few will enter!** What of: **the whole world wonders after the beast and worships his image.** Doesn't these statements say; what is most popular with man, is wrong in the eyes of God? Is this not the way, each time God has given a new covenant?

According to the <u>revelation</u> of the <u>mystery</u> which was <u>kept secret</u> for long ages but <u>is</u> <u>now</u> disclosed and <u>through</u> the <u>prophetic writings</u> is <u>made known</u> to <u>all nations,</u> according to the <u>command of the eternal God</u>, to bring about the <u>obedience of faith</u>--- to the only wise God be glory for evermore through Jesus Christ!

God <u>has consigned</u> all men to <u>disobedience</u> that He may have mercy upon all.

Blessed are you --- --- for <u>flesh and blood</u> <u>has not</u> revealed this to you, but My Father who is in heaven.

Brethren, take note: those who create dissensions and difficulties, in opposition to the doctrine which you have been taught; avoid them. For such persons do not serve our Lord Christ, but their own appetites and by fair and flattering words they deceive the hearts of the simple-minded. Jeremiah said, for both prophet and priest ply their trade through the land and have no knowledge.

Eldon Ward, as was with Apostle Paul, 2Corinthians 11:6 "even if I am unskilled in speaking, I am not in knowledge." --- The Lord said, the majority of people will not listen to God's truth, but will continually wonder after the beast. That beast being, 2Corinthians 10:12 "Not that we venture to class or compare ourselves with some of those who commend themselves. But when they measure themselves by one another and compare themselves with one another, they are without understanding."

Can there be any doubt that the Lord was speaking of hand-me-down-religion? Both old and new testaments say, "Those taught by God need no other teacher!" Would God teach a couple hundred different doctrines?

Denominational preachers "claim" to have been called of God to give His truth. Paul said church is in a man's house. Jesus gave the same calling to all true believers, "go into the highways and hedges and compel them to come." Contrary to popular belief, Jesus was speaking of coming to Him, personally in Spirit! Not to priest, preacher or denomination! The curtain has been torn in two!

The Lord's prime example of one (Philip) called to be a preacher (all true believers), was in showing another person the balance of the old prophets to Jesus.

Those that venture to class to learn the wisdom of men (in God's word) will not be taught by the Holy Counselor. For, they are displaying they do not believe the book of John, to which is blasphemy of Jesus and the Holy Spirit.

Therefore, God said they would not eat of the tree of life that they may live forever (flaming sword/Spirit of God). **"Where there is no prophecy the people <u>cast off</u> restraint, but <u>blessed is he who keeps the law</u>**

Since the time of Jesus, the majority of people have bought into the used-car-salesmanship of preachers. Yet they will not open the mouth of God and study. Or, if they should read, it is not the words of God they follow, but the perceived wisdom of educated men. **"Many will knock but few will enter."**

(JOHN) 6:45 **It is <u>written in the prophets</u>, "and <u>they shall all be taught by God</u>." <u>Everyone</u> who has <u>heard and learned from the Father</u>** (Spirit revealing God's truth through His word) **comes to me** (Jesus).

To those whom will humble themselves, with all sincerity, asking God for truth: A witness from Eldon Ward that the very Spirit of God still speaks to the mind of people. It is the foundation of Jesus' church. The prophetic writings is the mouth of God. **<u>Not taught</u> by <u>human wisdom</u> but taught by the Spirit, interpreting spiritual truths to those who possess the Spirit** (imagination is not spirit)!

The only way to possess God's Spirit is when one is completely convinced that **"every word out of the mouth of God"** is the only truth and dedicates life to it, through asking the Lord for understanding!

The first third of this book will be hard to absorb, but the further a person reads, the more light will shine. The author of this book is actually just one taking dictation from the Spirit of God. Therefore, all people that get hurt feelings from reading this book, or shameful feelings as this author did, don't get mad; search the scripture and history to "<u>Truthfully</u>" prove it wrong! Not just another opinion but, prove it wrong in the eyes of God!

Chapter 1

BEAST KINGDOM

1 Cor.15:39---<u>all flesh is not the same flesh</u>: **there is one kind of flesh of <u>men</u>, another flesh of <u>beasts</u>, another of <u>fishes</u>, and another of <u>birds</u>.** Truth of this statement, is taught by nature and through war. Animals do not form kingdoms, such as man does. However, men worship the creature more than the creator. Therefore, "Beast" would be as God taught, "spirit of men" (all about self, same as beasts) contrary to the Spirit of God (connected to all known things)! "Kingdom" is the controlling factor in the singular-mind-set of a group.

Though animals have ability to learn fearful and security, their foremost drive is in doing as they please to which is dictated by survival and reproduction. People are of the same order with an added ability to reason what has been, what is and enhance their future. From the very beginning man has chosen to leave off his ability to reason and live as an animal (all for self). Is it really any wonder that the <u>perceived</u> highly intelligent "claim" man to have derived from animals?

The Creator said, **in his generations, man is wiser than the children of Light.** Solomon said **the only thing a man has the right to take pride in, is the fruit from his labor.** Information is important; is all information life essential? Is, selling words from mouth, "labor"?

Jesus said **we will always have the poor with us.** Some people were given a life of inability to provide for themselves. This, Jesus said **to be for purposes of the Creator.** Man, for a big part, has always strived to make it through life the easiest way possible, even if it means walking on other people.

1

Some people use their own mind and do their own labor. Then there are two other mind-sets of reasoning. The perceived-highly-intelligent try to follow what their imagination says is the dominant animal of a herd. Scripture repeatedly tells us what one believes and continually follows, is their god. Therefore, the more subordinates, the bigger the god.

The truth of a dominate animal is a selection of either the strongest or has the most in-life-experience. Usually it is a combination of both. With man, it is a majority that choose a perceived-intelligent that crows the loudest.

Scoff all that you will. Then run to a building of seclusion with a man standing on a platform, above you, and say "AMEN" to every word he says. Or when it is time to select a leader of the people, go to the religious leaders or political-party-leaders or Masonic-temple to see how you are to vote. The leaders of these groups, for the most part, are made up from people that have a life-experience of going to school then selling words for a living. As God indicates; little to no labor with hands!

Then there is the mind-set of, "O, Woe is me, want someone please feel sorry for me!" Plain and simple dead-beat looking for a free ride through life. Giving a helping-hand, at times, is necessary and is brotherhood.

The first week of earth and all that pertains to it, was the Creator setting up good (God's will). From the "First" seventh day, man began to follow what his imagination told him of animals, instead of meditating on God. That is, some men have always done this, the majority have just mindlessly wondered after the supposed-highly-intelligent and worshipped (believing) the image portrayed.

God made man in His own likeness and placed him in a heaven on earth. God's likeness is a standard of mind-set and consciousness of all things. God did not want a well programmed robot, but a friend. This could only happen through freedom of choice.

God placed the **tree of life/let there be Light/Jesus**. To which is the likeness of God. He also placed the tree of knowledge of good and evil. To which is an individual's thing and not as a whole of all things. Then God: **took the man and put him in the garden. God commanded the man, saying, you may freely eat of every tree of the garden; but of the tree of the knowledge of good and evil you shall not eat.** It does not matter what the materialistic-thing may have been. But, choosing a way of life/ Freedom of choice!

Then God made woman. Evidently man told woman of all God had decreed. For, the animal talked to the woman. She said, **we may eat of the fruit of the trees, but God said you shall not eat of the fruit of the tree which is in the midst of the garden.**

At this time, the woman did not know of lying. The animal said, "You will not surely die." This being an attitude of individualism. ---One that thinks only of themselves will attempt to get others to follow their lead that themselves may be justified (become a god). The woman's choice was with the one she had not known. The man made the same choice by accepting the woman as his god.

Then the eyes of both were opened and they knew that they were naked. We know we are different individuals and we are indifferent to God. Satan was not created by God, but by man. Had the tree been left alone???

Then God said, **lest he put forth his hand and take also of the tree of life and eat and live forever.** Jesus said **we must eat His flesh and drink His blood** (Spirit/become the same as Him). -ALL the words of God must be fulfilled or He would be no different than the serpent.

"Because you have listened to the voice of your wife,"---"cursed is the ground because of you. ---Out of the ground you were taken. ---you are dust. ---to dust you shall return." The breath of life, to all living creatures, came from the breath of God. No breath will ever die! Some will return to God and some

3

will forever be in a lake of fire, away from God. All is recorded in scripture!

God made a stay of execution, for one, concerning the curse of the ground. **The voice of your brother's blood is crying to Me from the ground. And now you are cursed <u>from</u> the ground.**

At least three times, the scripture says to not trust your friend (their opinion at face value) nor to put your faith in a guide (preacher/ politician). One of the passages says do not even trust the spouse that has been with you from your youth. What is a personal relationship, other than one to one? If the number in "God's will" equaled man-church-membership: war and strife today???

For one studying in spirit for truth, the books of Job and John explains the above statements very clearly. However, for those that do not know how to study in spirit, the Creator through the old prophets has explained in the literal-materialistic. The fact is, very, very few people can understand either. Two factors cause this. One is those wanting to be perceived as having a closer connection to the Creator than does other people/a god. Second is simple-minded that allow the gods to do their reasoning for them. <u>True Believers are compelled</u>, by Holy Spirit, to recognize (cannot acquaint) God and His redemptive plan to others!

<u>Deception-Delusion</u>: This man could wish I were one that had heard about Jesus and accepted Him on blind faith. Because, the Lord said these are they that are truly blessed! However, God gave this man a life that has taught to prove out everything. Trying to prove God through human wisdom did not work. When life was driven to the pit of depression, only then was said, "If there is such a thing as an almighty God, "You" will have to prove it! For, very little was ever heard that could be convincing!"

From attending all of the different denominational-man-churches is found they are not different, but all the same! The Lord said to **not follow doctrines of men**; they all have one and none are the same as that of the Lord!

The denominations of man-church, in the time of Jesus' ministry said **He had not been to school to learn of God!** Paul said **he and the apostles did not venture to class to learn of God!** Peter, at the time of the Holy Spirit revealing God's Messiah to him, was just as much red-neck as is this man today; he had not even learned letters! Yet, most all of whom "claim" to have been called of God, to give His truth, have attended a bible college/ learned through human wisdom. Many even claim to have a doctoral degree in God's truth (something like equal to God?).

I had already, <u>three times</u>, read the scripture throughout. Therefore, when I again began reading the book of John, each passage was making more sense than ever before. Reason being, Jesus was bringing into remembrance all scripture of old and new testimonies that pertained to the particular teaching.

This man has never been in Israel and does not personally know anyone that is there or has been there. Yet, how do I know people in Israel, since 1948, have begun again in pagan worship? The old prophets spoke of after 1948! Only God's Spirit can give one understanding!

This man has yet to hear a preacher that does not speak a great amount through imagination or delusion. The very fact that they are denominational, says, they neither know God nor do they believe Him (**is this not why you are wrong, you know neither the scripture nor the power of God**). Jesus gave the example of a true preacher when He sent Philip to the dude riding in a chariot and studying Isaiah. Philip explained the teaching on through the fulfillment by Jesus. Philip did not pass a collection plate, but went on to the next task.

In the early days of America, this kind of preacher was called a circuit-rider and there was very few of them. This man has to wonder, if today, the collection plates were filled with chickens and jars of preserves, how long would it be before the gods of most preachers, would give them a different calling. IICor.2:17 **for we are not <u>like so many</u>; <u>peddlers</u> of God's word.**

The book of Job explains very well denominational preaching/ teaching of today. The words of Job and his three friends sounded reasonable. However, God was very displeased with them and would have destroyed them but for Job being a righteous man and giving sacrifice and repentance. Yet, God said nothing of the words of the young man "Elihu", to which indicates the words of Elihu is the words that should be used in recognizing God to other people.

Even though I have never seen a church-building built after the pattern in heaven (it must have been very important, as God was so strict about it), I can find nothing wrong with a building that a community can come together in, to discuss/study the scripture and praise God. I personally can see denominational-man-church as very little more than just retail-Jesus-business (With American Government Approval). Paul could only see; possibly one may hear of Jesus for the first time.

Another form: When the hurricanes hit the gulf coast. Many true disciples of Jesus, in this man's community, gathered needs for the afflicted. In order to find a distribution point, we began calling all organizations that advertise helping those in need. Each of these do-gooder-organizations told us they would not accept staples, but would accept money. Because, they "Could buy staples down there much cheaper". They must have thought they were talking to a total moron. It does not get any cheaper than free and the reason we are taking it to them is because there is no place left <u>down there</u> to buy anything! I understand support to keep operating: time of disaster everyone must give!

Is, just money, complete tithing? Brethren say most of world help comes from those in bargaining with God. To which, justifies our being judgmental of other people.

There are many well-meaning, God-fearing people that attend denominational churches! It is not this man's intent to condemn anyone; that is not my job nor authority. But I must try very hard to make people aware of how we are disobedient to Almighty

God! I did find denominational man-churches and National Guard command-post in Louisiana and Mississippi that would distribute several semi loads of help.

Door to Truth: Anyone that has done much history study, know governments are just a chip off the block of religion. I personally am a strong believer in separation of man-church from government. Because, each denomination is another political party. In the two government parties of U.S. is the same ending goal. One theme is to control people, thereby, controlling all money. The other is to control money, thereby, controlling all people.

Consider all religious orders in the twenty-first century. Deep research, reveals, the goal of ALL is to control the mind of all people on earth. God has always granted the wish of the majority! We must obey laws of our land; made by people we voted for! Kings will be of one mind and give their power to son of perdition for one hour!

The constitution of the United States was drawn up by the church that Jesus established. **Where two or more are gathered together in My name I will be there also.** The very fact that the Spirit of God revealed to Peter that Jesus is the Christ of God, is the rock Jesus built His church on! Did you get it??? The Spirit of God talked to a man! NOT, Peter, nor any man, but the Holy Spirit speaking God's truth to a person's mind, is the rock of the foundation: A personal relationship! There is no go between! **The truth will set you free.** Not set you free from sin. "Set you free from deception". Sin will still be an option until The Day of the Lord. It is why Jesus died on a cross: each time we recognize our disobedience to God and make a pact with God, through Jesus, to do our best to never again be in the same thought or act, God wipes it from His mind. Come judgment day, there will be nothing on God's mind that we can be judged for. Jesus said, **you have a judge and that judge is the words I have spoken!** To which, better than ninety percent of His words came right out of the old testimonies! Deuteronomy18:15-19

Literal-Visual: Many times Jesus would give a parable teaching to the public then go deeper with the twelve trainees and then ask, **"Do you still not understand."** It is the same today. Multitudes upon multitudes of people claim to know God and His Christ, but cannot see past their nose on a clear day. Daniel 10:12 **then He said to me, fear not, Daniel, for from the first day that you <u>set your mind</u> to <u>understand</u> and <u>humbled</u> yourself before <u>your God</u>, your words have been heard.** Jeremiah 33:3 **call to Me and I will answer you and will tell you <u>great</u> and <u>hidden things</u> which <u>you have not known</u>.** ---This man can give a God's-love witness that God is the same today! Furthermore, God's own begotten Son gave the supreme sacrifice that I will not have to pay for past, present nor future sins. John 11:51 *he did not say this of his own accord, <u>but being high priest that year he prophesied</u> that <u>Jesus should die</u> for the nation and not for the nation only, but to gather into one the <u>children of God</u> who are scattered abroad.*

Throughout the old testimonies God has said, **you will understand clearly in the latter days.** Also, **this pertains to the time of the end.** Jesus said, **if you do not understand things on earth how can you understand things in heaven.**

So very many people have told this man that these things do not matter, just believe in Jesus. Throughout life I have found opinions to be very poorly based. I cannot believe in something that I know nothing about. Furthermore, God has told me the same thing: **study to show thyself approved, a workman unto God. - Lean not unto thy own understanding, but look to the Lord and He shall direct thy paths. - Continue to grow in grace and knowledge.**

One passage of scripture says, **men will run to and fro in the earth looking for knowledge and <u>knowledge will be increased</u>.** A second passage of scripture says, **men will run to and fro in**

the earth looking for <u>knowledge and there will be none</u>. With a matter being put so seriously, should not all people be searching for the truth? It will not be found from preacher nor priest!

The second passage, this man will (God willing) attempt to point the direction in the book with seven seals, for that is the time of its happening. The first passage is now! For, multitudes of people today, are jumping from one man-church to another, looking for some preacher they can believe in (Not going to happen!). I have met several strangers in the past ten years that have said the exact same things that the Spirit has revealed to this man. It is not the same as hand-me-down-preaching, but all scripture will balance and history is a witness.

Chapter 2

BEGINNING FEAR

For generations, the GREAT IMAGE in Nebuchadnezzar's dream, has been continually preached down to its feet. Some have even guessed that Jesus is the rock that hit's the image in the feet. However, I have never heard a truthful preaching of the fact that God changed Nebuchadnezzar from king of men to king of beast, nor a truthful preaching on the feet and toes of the great image. These things can only be known from deep study and the Spirit's guidance.

The great image is all one structure, made from several different materials. God has explained to us where one material ended and another began. The part where two materials are mixed together (iron & clay), God left for us to be a workman unto God, for all is recorded in history.

The <u>feet</u> was Rome beginning its fall; it was hiring mercenaries for its defense; the same as the United States is doing today. When people grow tired of their government- officials playing god over the efforts of the people; as far as government decisions are concerned, there is no more patriotism. Is there not talk of states breaking away from the union? To which is just a smaller god. People need to grow into adults and stand for what God gave and patriots defended! Politicians have enacted themselves a healthy retirement after one term. While making it hard for a war veteran to even get medical help. The old war tactic: divide and conquer. If people truly loved God and country, they would do all in their power to preserve the earned freedoms!

The way we know fulfillment of scripture-prophecy is by comparing history to prophecy. Did the Lord not tell us; **in the**

latter days you will understand clearly. Each time a prophecy fulfillment is revealed to this man, it makes my belief and faith in God grow stronger.

How do we know it is the latter days? Isaiah said the Messiah would be in the latter days. Peter stood up and said, **these men are not drunk, it is as the prophet Joel said, in the latter days** (God has always given a small sample before the big happening)! Also, there are many prophecy points to happen after Messiah and the majority have been fulfilled. Earth's judgment began in the latter days (recorded in scripture)! By the end of this little book, direction will be pointed to fulfillments as well as how to recognize some that have yet to be fulfilled.

The Lord said there are no apostles and no prophets from God today. However, an elder in heaven told John, **"Worship God, for the testimony of Jesus is the spirit of prophecy"**. When Jesus went back to heaven He was seated on the throne beside God. The Almighty then gave all records to Jesus and charge of all things to Him. Now, He even knows the Father's final day of earth time. Furthermore, Jesus now has authority of all words in scripture; **let there be light** and Jesus began to shine---**all things were created for Jesus and because of Him they were created.** ---Is the Spirit beginning to speak?

Toes---The whole Roman Empire was made from ten barbaric tribes of people. When the Roman Empire dissolved, all ten tribes formed their own nation and government (seven Western European nations). However, within Italy another government was set up on a hundred and nine acres, making it the smallest country on earth.

At first it was head-quartered on the black sea. It was formed by die-hard-politicians through a thought-process of Emperor Constantine. It was called "papal Rome" that it might draw in honorary members from sympathizers in all countries formed from the fall of Rome.

By the year of moving the headquarters to its present location in Italy, papal Rome had completely destroyed three of the original ten barbaric tribes (supposedly in the name of God), they are found nowhere in the world today.

The little country/kingdom was named Vatican City and is the mother of all denominational-church today. You say no! For, the preacher says we are not in protest. Exactly right!---All have a building of seclusion (none built by heaven's pattern), all have a man-doctrine, everyone that does not agree with the doctrine is banished, all have a man standing on a platform above the people and his word is gospel! All disagreeing (his word is gospel), is banished!

All denominations of man-church follow some of Constantine's **"thought" to change God's times and law.**--All, decree that a person has to come to the priest/preacher declaring they have sinned and be sprinkled or dunked before they can be a registered member of the congregation. If the person gets a disagreeable-attitude they can be banished (is this not the leaders now hold the book-of-life and can write in or blot out any name they desire?) This has no part in scripture! It is the very same as any other weird occult, started by one man or a small group. **They will be so strong if it were possible would even fool the very elect.**

The Lord left prophecy points that denominational-man-church would pick up: denying foods, denying marriage, denying the Sabbath, claiming God to be the author of confusion, calling men father, displaying graven images, preach to a red-neck in the tongue of Latin, etc., etc. ---A man seeing a snake that he truly believes to be poisonous, does he put his face in front of the snake? One either believes God or they do not! Taking what one likes of God and throwing the rest away is becoming one's own god.

Do we have the seal of God or the mark of the beast? People tell this man, God is not so nit-picky. God told this man, He **is very jealous and shares His glory with no one!** Furthermore, God said **those that have stolen will not enter heaven less**

they repent and pay back all they have stolen. I will leave this deciphering to preachers/ politicians; it comes under the leaven of the Pharisees.

Beguiled: Preachers "claim" Jesus to have done away with God's law. The scripture this man studies, says, Jesus **did away with legalistic bonds** that had been activated by denominational-man-church. (A god having to backtrack and apologize cannot be God over this man!) Jesus said to **live by every word that came out of the mouth of God.** The Almighty said **the way He was at the time of Jesus' death, was the same as the first day of creation, and will be the same on The Day of The Lord!** (Is truth only what one comes up with in the moment?)

From the mid-nineteen-hundreds to the turn of the century, there was a man preaching Jesus to the world. I felt the man was very sincere about Jesus, humble and concerned for the salvation of people. However, I was concerned of how to feel about the closing of his speeches, saying, "Be sure to go to church next Sunday". Also, his visits to the office of the son of perdition. God does not compromise, but He does not charge us for what we do not yet understand (Jesus' grace).

Jesus is speaking of deception that only the elect can see, in Revelations 2:23-24 **I am He which searcheth the reins and hearts** (way of life): **and I will give unto every one of you according to your works** (toward God's doctrine). **But unto you I say and unto the rest in Thyatira, as many as have not this doctrine and which have not known the depths of satan, as they speak; I will put upon you none other burden".**

(Just don't try to learn; we will be alright? Guess again! **God consigned all men to disobedience that He may have mercy upon all!** We were born into sin. It is our responsibility to overcome!) As is all when first born, Adam was innocent. Second day of life, Adam was age of accountability. As was with all things, God gave Adam choice for all men.

Blasphemy: At the same time there was a TV-doctorial-preacher that has published many religious books (to me is wholesale-Jesus-business). However, at the time, I did not know as much about the depths of satan as what the Spirit has taught me to this point. So, I tuned him in, a lot. That is, until one Sunday he said, "Sure, Saturday is the true Sabbath, but if we change back now, it would disrupt the entire world".

My first thought was, did not the Lord say He was going to disrupt the entire world because of disobedience? Then scripture came to mind that the Jews were convicted of their sin of marrying into different nationalities of people. They were so convicted that they put away their wives and kids! But we gentiles cannot even change from pagan Sabbath. What is definition of "obedience"? Are we sure definition of "grace"? Why did God even bother to explain good and evil?

How could the guy know the true Sabbath, less the Holy Spirit direct him to it? What did Jesus say about blasphemy of the Holy Spirit? For many years, death put no fear in this man, yet, I was not going to tell the Almighty that He will just have to get over His bad self!

And He said to man, "Behold, the fear of the Lord, that is wisdom; and to depart from evil is understanding." Sabbath made for man to meditate God!

Many people say this is the legalistic bonds that I talk about. Maybe so! However, Isaiah said **the Sabbath would be held for ever in the new heaven and in the new earth.** Therefore, I think I will get practiced up while on this earth. Paul said, after the apostles were gone, we would have to work out our own salvation. I do not label myself by any name. Such as "Christen, Judaism, Moslem" to which has a sound of "self has locked into God". My life is dedicated to pleasing God. The only way I see possible is by imitating what I understand of Jesus. For, He is with God and with man! **His delight will be in pleasing God!**

Stiff-Necked: One final conclusion on subject: God gave the Jew two chances to be world leader. Then He gave charge to the gentile (remember the parable of pruning the branches from the cultivated olive tree (Jew) and grafting in the wild olive branches (gentile). He said gentiles should not get high-minded because, He could do another pruning and graft the Jew back into the cultivated stump. This is exactly what God did in 1948 (If U.S. was right with God, would we have been pruned?). Joel said it best: **hear this, you aged men** (last men on earth), **give ear all inhabitants of the land! Has such a thing happened in your days or in the days of your fathers** (Noah & sons): a people that came from no nation to being a nation three times! (Vatican City& many other nations twice) However, God said He did not bring Jews back a final time because they had finally got it right but, He did it for **the sake of His great name!** When this has had serious study, it should be obvious that no organizations of people are right with God! It can only be truth of God through a one person relationship to God!

Since 1948, the Jews have already proved God's truth in the matter, **"Woe unto him who keeps his sword from blood, who keeps his sword sheathed"**. Many Jew men have restarted the Pharisee-man-denomination-church, refusing to take up arms for Israel; looking for a free ride through life. Abraham, Joshua and David were all kings, priest and warriors! This same "freeloading attitude" was in the United States during the Nam-era and still even stronger today; the stage is set!

Chapter 3

DEPTHS OF SATAN

The cause, of people that have already and will lose their soul, is in not choosing obedience to God (who is His children). When one truly chooses God, they cannot help but to become aware of Jesus (Ex.23:20)! Disobedience is what caused the Jew to not understand Jesus nor God's will in sending Jesus.

Gentiles, for the most part, just follow the ones that crow the loudest. Especially if the crowers have a signed piece of paper that says they are smart. Simply put, the majority of gentiles prefer someone else doing their thinking for them; even though, the majority will claim to be their own person! If we are not honest with our self, how can we possibly think we are honest with God? People that have no conscience cannot ever know God! Is faith, in God, or in man-words?

More deception from the seculars: From the beginning of the industrial age, there has been a world-wide organization of supposed Christian men. Supposedly their agenda is having fun and helping sick children. As a young man I had considered joining. Because, it had a lot of well-meaning-members that were my friends. However, I must know the truth of a matter before I can take part. **Do not put your faith or trust in a friend or guide.**

I found the organization to have a hierarchy of hidden agenda that is kept from the majority of the members. It is a pyramid system with an agenda to over through liberty and justice for all. Which is to over through the Constitution of the United States. The general public would be very surprised to know how many of our presidents and legislators were and are members.

The foremost code is, <u>members do for members first</u>, to which most all elections and best jobs are <u>controlled</u>. The foremost agenda, of the hierarchy, is to <u>control</u> the flow of all money throughout the world, thereby, <u>controlling</u> people. There are members from both political parties and from all denominations of religion.

There are several small organizations, in every city, that hold the same interest and some work together with other cities. The most tail-telling sign of these agendas is not allowing women to enter the assemblies. **When they say I am in the secret chamber, believe it not!**

Many Jews and Gentiles have strong desire to know God in truth. If it were not so, this man would not waste time writing or speaking. However, I have struggled with the fact that God declared: people did not listen to His prophets nor to Jesus' apostles. So, who is this man that people would listen to me? But the Lord said I must give testimony!

I have no misguided delusions that this little book might become highly accepted. However, if it points the right path for a few, it will have been worthwhile.

One must come to understanding that satan has a counterfeit for everything God has decreed. Satan works his magic through the ignorance of people. Ignorance comes from two factors. One, is believing one's self to be highly intelligent. The other, is believing we have no intelligence. Education =subject lived or studied, Intelligent =no mistakes. Reasoning =present-situation compared to similarities of proven truth. God holds blameless, those that have not and those that will never reach age-of accountability.

Jesus and later the apostles said <u>perdition/ lawlessness was already at work</u>. God said, **if I were to write My law by the ten-thousand he would think it a strange thing**. One must have a conscience in order to have understanding. Every thought or act we have must fit within the Ten Commandments, or it will be lawlessness/perdition. If God had written His law in the ways of man, it would be programing a robot. Even in U.S., man is but a puppet on superior's string.

This statement of Jesus and the apostles was not something new. For God said, **the scribe's false pen.** Which today, is for sure running out of control. Most all denominational-man-churches have printed their own interpretation of scripture or taken one and supplement the margins with delusion.

NOTE: Many of God's teachings that have been hidden from the foundation of the world, comes in groups of three (Joseph said, when it comes twice it is sure and soon).

Jesus said, **"Where two or more are gathered together in My name, I will be there also."** Man-church uses this statement to justify its assemblies. God said the great temple in Jerusalem would **be called a house of prayer.** Jesus said **your house will be left unto you desolate.** What is desolate, but a place where God is not?

Furthermore, this tells this man that the visual-materialistic-temple will never again be built on the temple-mound in Jerusalem. If God has nothing more to do with the building He supplied the blueprints for, will He be in the houses built by men, claiming to be for God? However, we must be careful that satan <u>not</u> get us into chasing rabbits through the scripture and loose the point of God's truth.

<u>Foremost point being: the scripture.</u> God desired to walk on earth with man. God cannot be in the presents of sin. Signified by, **"My God, My God, why has thou forsaken Me."** All sin of the world, by those desiring to be with God, was on Jesus. God loves the light/Jesus and He made man for Jesus. Therefore, Jesus had power to leave sin in the pit (cursed ground). John 10: **so there shall be one flock, one shepherd. For this reason the Father loves Me, because I lay down My life, that I may take it again. No one takes it from Me, but I lay it down of My own accord.**

I have power to lay it down and I have power to take it again; this charge I have received from My Father.

God had already decreed that **in the day man sins, he will surely die:** Jesus took the sin of the blameless: **he who believes in Me will never die** (Breath/spirit)! ---The Lord considers, **a day is as a thousand years.** Noah's grandpa lived over nine-hundred years and died in the world flood. God's proof: one thousand years with Jesus!

During the time from the first sin to earths cleansing, some **men called upon the name of the Lord.** Afterwards, God preordained men to be born that would humble themselves and set their minds to know God that He may teach the world through them. This did not work, so He sent the Light. This would not work forever unless Jesus was ever present. So God sent His Spirit!

Abraham was thirty-eight years of age when Noah died. At that time, history was carried forth by hand-me-down word-of-mouth. Moses was, by decree of God, raised by a people that had always been infested by angels, to which had left their proper place. **All knowledge comes from God!** The Egyptians had been taught to read and write.

NOTE: many man-churches teach the fallen angels to have died in the world-flood. Before the flood, angels had made children with daughters of men. The offspring were called "mighty men". After the flood, Nimrod "was the first of the mighty men."

Man, reading and writing was not of God's plan. If it had been, would He not give to Abram first? Had man been obedient from the beginning, there would have been no need of so-called "formal education", for all needs were already met.

Even though formal education was defiantly brought into the world, God turned satan's evil into some good for man. The trials and failures were recorded as history that future man might use his power of reasoning to keep from disobedience to God.

However, from man's youth, his desire is to do his own thing/ evil. Formal education is the foremost tool in men becoming gods. Even in use of the scripture.

Groups of three: the first recorded scripture was in Egyptian, then Arabic, then Hebrew. After this, the scripture was translated into the Greek, with some of the New Testament being first recorded in the Greek. From there it was translated into many different tongues. Each translation was done by one man or a family or one denomination of religion, which was one god at the head.

King James of England was so stressed by all the bickering over whose translation was right (same as denominational-church) that he assembled a panel of scholars to search original recordings. He decreed a translation to be made as close to the original records as possible, in the English tongue. **Where two or more are gathered together in My name I will be there also.** No doubt in this man's mind, Jesus, set-up the scenario and sent God's Spirit into the minds of the scholars that the translation would be approved by God: He will not leave us!

Since that time, satan has been working over-time. His supposed-highly-intelligent-followers rewrote into the supposed words in use today. God is always a step ahead!

The ancient Egyptians, Greeks and Romans used the pith of the stem of a tall marsh plant to make writing paper. It grew in southern Europe and the Nile valley. In the 1870's Greek papyrus was found in Egypt. There was all sorts of documents, such as would be found in a district courthouse. Showing a common Greek was used in the Roman Empire until maybe the 5th.-6th. Century.

A group of Godly men have matched the "dead sea scrolls" and other finds to the King James for clarity. **Where two or more are gathered together in My name I will be there also.**

Even so, one has to be very alert to what is being read. Many books claim to be King James Version, but on close inspection, they are rewrites to cash in on the wholesale-god-business. Unapproved scripture will bring confusion in searching noted scripture in this book.

One of many Examples: the counterfeit Rev.14:4 these are they which were not defiled with women; for they are virgins. In **Jesus approved** King James Scripture: **It is these who have not defiled themselves with women, for they are chaste.** First of all, God gave woman as a gift to man (a help mate). Man is to be provider and protector of woman. Together, they are one.

The definition of **chaste** was given by Jesus at the wedding feast. Mary had been told before she conceived Jesus that He would be the Son of God. Therefore, she knew His power before the feast. When she probed Jesus to straighten out the disaster, HE let her know He was a man and God had decreed woman would not have authority over man; **Jesus was chaste**.

However, today, in the United States: **they have entered the houses and confound the silly women.** To the point, they believe it is alright to ignore the prophets and apostles and become scripture teachers/preachers, politicians/making laws, law arbitrators, military leaders, even commander in chief of the armed forces.

Is it not bad enough with those of appearance to men, but will not (in ten life times) serve their country, but are commander in chief of full grown men. (What sane man would desire to kill people?) What makes preacher/ politician above full grown men? "Formal Education"? Why not have strongest and most-in-life-experience? If we are going to live like animals, let us go whole hog! Amen???

God said and **seven women will come to one man, for his name, that their reproach may be hidden.** For the fact that woman admitted she had been beguiled, where man blamed the woman, if woman holds to God's decree for women, she will not be held accountable for world-sin as will be with men! God doesn't miss anything!

Chapter 4

FALSE PROPHET

There are many false prophets today. The United States has two that sprang up denominational-man-churches. One is a woman that published her dead husband's transcripts, in her own name.

This man prays Jesus, to send the Holy Counselor to each that may read this writing. **"Continue to grow in grace and knowledge"**---the word "continue" says this man does not know all the depth of satan. What this man does know, must be studied in the scripture. For, if it does not come from God's Spirit, then it will be registered in another's mind in a <u>form of delusion</u>.

<u>Such as</u> those taking Joel's prophecies to be in this day and age. To which, is saying Jesus did not fulfill all of God and the apostles did not fulfill all of Jesus. People prophesying again, was God talking about the thousand year rule and rein with Jesus: check-out what has to take place before people will prophesy again!

<u>For now</u>--- **the coming of the lawless one by the <u>activity of satan</u> will be with <u>all power</u> and with <u>pretended signs</u> and wonders and with <u>all wicked deception</u> for those who are to perish.**

The fulfilled prophecies tell the wise that <u>Judaism/ Zionist</u> has not gotten right with God and the same is true with the order that claims <u>Christianity</u>. Still there is a third claiming God, but is a total <u>counterfeit/false prophet</u>.

After the apostles, there are no more prophecies from God, in this age. It is recorded in the scripture. Therefore, in 622 A.D. rose up one claiming to be a prophet and wrote of himself as a near copy of Jesus. Even, supposedly, rising from the temple-mound in Jerusalem, going to be with God. God is a trinity. Satan has a counterfeit.

However, the false prophet left out a few parts. **"It is appointed unto man once to die"** (dust body). Jesus was a flesh man, on earth, and He died. Jesus told us Elijah died in the form of John the baptizer. I cannot back it up with definite scripture (each must decide for them self); my perception is, Enoch to have died in the form of Stephan. There was no genealogy of Stephan and at death, he had the face of an angel (Remember: Moses coming down the mountain, after being with God; he wore a veil because of the brightness of his face). Furthermore, he had given an account of scripture as if he held queue-cards. There is another great factor about Stephan, to be covered in a latter chapter.

The main point of subject: **the lawless one will make a secret pack with the false prophet and overnight many armies will fall** (recorded in Daniel). I know, for now they appear to be total opposites. Israel will be the last stand against them. (I know, opposite of preachers)

All three of these orders of people came about from disobedience to the Almighty God, through perceived high-intelligence (intelligence is a world apart from faith or conscience). Then **the <u>whole world</u> wondered after the beast and worshipped his image.** Those claiming to have no god, is false. For they have placed themselves in the position of a god. Also, **will receive the mark in the forehead and on the hand.** This too will be pointed out in a latter chapter. As Jesus taught, <u>without a solid foundation,</u> all will be lost/cannot be understood.

For those with a desire to save their soul, it is most important to understand Revelation 14:9 **if any one worships the beast and its image and receives a mark on his forehead or on his hand, he also shall drink the wine of God's wrath, poured unmixed into the cup of His anger and he shall be tormented with fire and brimstone in the <u>presence</u> of the <u>holy angels</u> and in the <u>presence</u> of the <u>Lamb</u>. The smoke of their torment goes**

up for ever and ever; they have no rest day or night, these worshippers of the beast and its image and whoever receives the <u>mark of its name</u>. Here is a call for the endurance of the <u>saints</u>, <u>those who keep the commandments</u> of God and <u>the faith of Jesus</u>.
I know preachers spew their delusion across the world but, have you, daily, searched the scripture to see if what he says is truth? Remember: **so strong if it were possible would even fool the very elect.** Elect, have been taught by God/Holy Spirit/Spirit of God (truth will set you free from deception). All others are delusion from God or deception of satan.

Did you register the definition of a saint? Saint, is God's word for one that is held <u>blameless</u>. Christen, is a word dreamed up by scoffers for those repeating Jesus' teachings. Does not necessarily mean a person tries to live within God's commandments nor that they have faith in Jesus.

Most man-churches (where "Christen" is claimed) require a person to stand between the congregation and the man (chosen by congregation) purporting to be Jesus or one of the apostles and repeat words. Then their name will be recorded in the book of life. ---<u>NOT</u> in the scripture this man studies!

When one has truly chosen the commandments of God and faith in Jesus as path of their life, they cannot help but to tell every one of the great peace and freedom in heart and mind! It is as Jesus told the preacher; **if these people do not proclaim the truth then the rocks will cry out.** Personally, how can a person stand before the Lord and explain the rocks doing their talking?

<u>Judaism/Zionist</u> claim the old wall, so-called <u>Christian-church</u>---<u>Moslem</u> has the temple-mound---and are all within a couple of blocks to each other in Jerusalem (all are as the dude the donkey talked to). Revelations 16:13 **I saw, issuing from the mouth of the <u>dragon</u> and from the mouth of the <u>beast</u> and from the mouth of the <u>false prophet</u>, three foul spirits like frogs; for <u>they are demonic spirits</u>, <u>performing signs</u>, who go abroad to**

the kings of the whole world, to assemble them for battle on the great day of God the Almighty. ---then there is God's remnant!

This was a short drive through the depths of satan. However, it would not matter how much a man says, unless the Holy Spirit is allowing a person to receive it in God's truth and there is only one way that will happen.

Chapter 5

SON OF PERDITION

Revelation 13. **I saw a beast rising out of the <u>sea</u>, with <u>ten horns</u> and <u>seven heads</u>, with <u>ten diadems</u> upon its horns and a <u>blasphemous name</u> upon its heads.** The prophets told us many symbols of representation that God uses (such a small thing to bring great delusion on high-intelligence). ---

Sea/water =people,
Horns =king/kingdom,
Heads =king/kingdom,
Diadems =king/crown/God's will,
Grass =people,
Blasphemy =claiming to be equal or completely denying. It is one of the reasons we must be studying from scripture approved by Jesus. The main reason is that both old and new testimonies says to not change any scripture. (God has not foretold anything that man has not attempted)

Rev.17:15 **the <u>waters</u> (sea) that you saw, where the harlot is seated, <u>are peoples and multitudes and nations and tongues.</u> The <u>ten horns</u> that you saw, <u>they</u> and the <u>beast</u> will hate the harlot; they will make her desolate and naked and devour her flesh (literally) and burn her up with fire, for <u>God has put it into their hearts</u> to carry out His purpose <u>by being of one mind</u> and giving over their royal power to the beast, until the words of God shall be fulfilled. The <u>woman</u> that <u>you saw</u> is <u>the great city</u> which <u>has dominion</u> over the kings of the earth.** Remember: the fourth beast is different from the others.

NOTE: God places kings; God just said kings have no chance of knowing God's truth. Therefore, do not put your faith and trust in a president.

NOTE: the golden image that Nebuchadnezzar set up, is still prominent today; when people hear bells ringing, organ playing, or gospel music they flock to the image.

Many times in the Old Testament, God spoke of Israel whoring after gods other than their own God. Gentiles are no different. Rev. 17:5 **Babylon the great, mother of harlots** --- the great image of Nebuchadnezzar's dream is a representation of all foreign gods that accumulated into the world powers from Babylon through Rome Empire and settled in papal Rome, with a little touch of Jesus and is taught throughout the world today. --- **And of earth's abominations. I saw the woman, drunk with the blood of the saints and the blood of the martyrs of Jesus.** ---**The beast that you saw was, and is not and is to ascend from the bottomless pit and go to perdition;** (1789AD. General Berthiar imprisoned the pope (leader of papal Rome: last of great image) in Valance South France where he died in the same year. Napoleon said Rome is finished forever. However, Jesus said, Rev. 2:20 **woman Jezebel, who calls herself a prophetess and is teaching and beguiling My servants to practice immorality and to eat food sacrificed to idols. I gave her time to repent, but she refuses to repent of her immorality.**

Prophet =statements never before used,
Food =teaching/doctrines,
Wine =teaching/doctrine,

1929AD. Presser put on by the United States; Mussolini reinstated the office of the pope and gave back all land and properties. American newspapers headlined, "Wound is Healed".

CAUTION: II Thess. 2. **Now concerning the coming of our Lord Jesus Christ and our assembling to meet Him, we beg you, brethren, not to be quickly shaken in mind or excited, either by spirit or by word, or by letter purporting to be from us** (apostles), **to the effect that the day of the Lord has come. Let no one deceive you in any way; for that day will not come, unless the rebellion comes first** (Mark 13:14 *when you see the desolating sacrilege set up where it ought not to be)* **and the man of lawlessness is revealed, the son of perdition, who opposes and exalts himself against every so-called god or object of worship,** ---any teaching contrary to the will of God is perdition. It is in all denominational and evangelical religion. The head that was wounded unto death, then came back to life, tells us by what office the son of perdition will arrive. Popes are perdition leaders, voted in by men. The man of lawlessness will take office through bribery; recorded in Daniel--- **so that he takes his seat in the temple of God** (I Corinthians 6:19 *do you not know that your body is a temple of the Holy Spirit within you, which you have from God?* (Heart & mind, faith & conscience in God's word) John13:6 Jesus said to him, *"I am the way and the truth and the life; no one comes to the Father, but by Me"* (one, only comes to Jesus if they are taught by God/Spirit revealing). A third materialistic temple being built on the temple-mound in Jerusalem, is a figment of people's imagination/delusion. It is the spiritual temple of David that will be rebuilt/a heart of love for God. --- **proclaiming himself to be god. You know what is restraining him now so that he may be revealed in his time**. ---I have said this book will not be widely accepted, because God has decreed, **"he may be revealed in "his time"/**time of happening (However, those taught by God: **Holy counselor will tell you things to come**).

John 16:12 Jesus said, **"I have yet many things to say to you, but you cannot bear them now** (Remember: baskets of fragments taken up after Jesus fed the multitudes and Jesus said, *see that none is lost*) when the Spirit of truth comes, He will **guide you** into **all the truth**; for He will **not** speak on His own authority, but whatever He hears He will speak and **He will declare to you the things that are to come**'.

NOTE: if what someone says, will not balance with scripture, it is false! *"Worship God, for the testimony of Jesus is the spirit of prophecy".*

---**For the mystery of lawlessness is already at work; only he** (satan) **who now restrains it will do so until he** (satan) **is out of the way.** --- Many preachers say "he" is Jesus. (My Jesus will never be out of the way!) The truth is in scripture, but most cannot see it because of being indoctrinated into deception/delusion. Who is the deceiver, who is his son? ---**Then the lawless one will be revealed and the Lord Jesus will slay him with the breath of His mouth and destroy him by His appearing and His coming.** (remember: evil cannot be in presents of the LIGHT) **coming** of the **lawless one** (today) **by the activity of satan will be with all power** and **pretended signs** and **wonders** and with **all wicked deception** for those who are to perish, because they **refused to love the truth** and so be saved. **Therefore God sends upon them a strong delusion, to make them believe what is false, so that all may be condemned who did not believe the truth but had pleasure in unrighteousness.** (claiming God but, denying the power of God) Repeating words, a dip in the big tub, on church rolls, will not save souls. This very thing is where many will be knocking on Jesus' door and He will not open. Remember: Noah in the ark and water rising.

Golden Image: Amazing to this man, the number of preachers whom speak of the rock hitting the great image in the feet and saying the rock to be Jesus. However, they do not have a clue as

29

to what is being destroyed. If it were possible to momentarily have a love for God's truth, they would know the destruction was coming on themselves and those that take the preacher's word as the gospel. Today, when people hear bells ringing, organ playing, gospel music, they flock to the golden image! Even threat of death could not make Daniel, Shadrach, Meshach, nor Abednego worship (believing) man-church. **What has been, will be!**

This not to say, all who attend man-church will be lost, not even all preachers! All depends on the truth of one's heart for God! It is difficult to have a clean heart when it is fed garbage. It does say the whole world is wondering after the beast and worshipping his image.

The angel will not place mark or seal until the lawless one arrives or until the point of death on the individual. Foretold signs says time is short. Regardless of God's appointed time, law of averages says this man has a short time. If God finds me blessed to miss the great tribulation: Praise God!

When this man first made total trust to God through faith that Jesus would stand up for me, before God, I also thought the Spirit was telling me to be a denominational preacher. It was spirit, but not the spirit one should want to follow. As I also, had a lot of indoctrination in deception. Very quickly, the Holy Spirit showed me that a man-church-preacher has to be a very good politician: straddle a five-barbed-wire-fence and not get a stitch in his pants. There is no God "and". It is "either, or"! God or mammon. Second, no man can teach God's truth! (That would be blasphemy) Man can only point the way to truth! Scripture through the Holy Spirit! Then I saw all people whom have the heart of David for God, have the same calling: **"go into the highways and hedges and compel them to come"** come to Jesus. The individual that chooses God, the Spirit will teach through study of scripture!

For those that rely on the Spirit for understanding, will soon have understanding of the seal of God and the mark of the beast. Jeremiah 1:16 **I will utter My judgments against them for all**

their wickedness in <u>forsaking Me</u>; they have burned incense to other gods and worshipped the <u>works of their own hands</u>. Church, Preacher, Spouse, children, homes, vehicles, money, land, etc., etc., anything to which a person <u>believes them self</u> to have achieved (burning incense to Baal (self).

James 2:24 **you see that a man is justified by works and <u>not</u> by faith alone.** A person can have all faith possible in Jesus, but <u>not</u> living within the will of God, is vanity/lost soul. <u>Jews stay on one side</u> and <u>gentiles on the other side</u>. Jews nor Gentiles can see; David was anointed to battle those of a mind-set contrary to the will of God. Jesus was sent to make known the very deception taught against God's will; that each may be God's anointed servant. True faith produces works!

Chapter 6

END OF COVENANTS

Ezekiel 1:4 **four living creators** Rev.4:6 **round the throne, on each side of the throne, are four living creatures, full of eyes in front and behind** ---Ezekiel and John saw these in heaven. Jesus said, **if you do not know things of earth how can you know things of heaven?** Both Ezekiel and John were believers of God and both were in the Spirit/studying or meditating on what they knew of God. <u>Example</u>: Daniel 9:2 **I, Daniel, perceived <u>in the books</u> the <u>number of years</u> which, according to the word of the Lord to Jeremiah the prophet, <u>must pass</u> before the <u>end</u> of the <u>desolations</u> of <u>Jerusalem</u>, namely, <u>seventy years</u>.** "Believing" is God's definition of worship. We must study in spirit to receive truth. Reading or blindly believing what is heard will bring delusion.

Every man-church with a street-bulletin says, "Worship at such & such a time". All man-churches hold the same worship: a little singing, then listening to a man giving his opinion of scripture/God---and congregations take the speech as the gospel. Is this not believing a man? So, who is being worshipped?

The majority of people in all congregations will claim to be Christen. If the scripture has already been studied, why would one have to have it read to them? Or as Jesus said, why do you think you need a doctor (we are to help provide a living (not make rich) for those that go to the sick/recognizing Jesus)? The only way one would know the preacher had it right, would be if the Spirit had already given truth. So why waste time in a building instead of being in the highways and hedges (one's daily life)? In other words: where is your power of reasoning? Know the truth of, "assemble thy selves" (it only takes two)!

Genesis 1:17-19 is the ruler of day and night: Second was things that live in water and things that fly in the first heaven: Third came all creatures that live on land: Fourth came man: **and let them have dominion over the fish of the sea and over the birds of the air and over cattle and over all the earth**---God gave man everything that has the breath of life (1 Cor.15:39 **for not all flesh is alike, but there is one kind for <u>men</u>, another for <u>animals</u>, another for <u>birds</u> and another for <u>fish</u>.** (Enmity between her seed & seed of any non-human). But, **man would rather worship the creature instead of the creator.** We are <u>new creatures</u> in Christ!

God has placed around His throne four living Spirits to place a particular order for each of His creations. Three live by a natural order or instinct. Man of today, calls this "mother nature". However, man was given the power of reasoning that he may be in the image of God. God did not want just another well programmed robot, but a friend to commune with in the cool of the evening. But God cannot be in presents of sin! Can those having pleasure in unrighteousness be in the second heaven?

<u>Man was not chaste.</u> Had he been, he may not have allowed something to change the words of scripture (not surely die). But, can we be for sure, with God saying, **"He consigned all men to disobedience that He may have mercy upon all."** But, then again, those who will be with the Lord for ever and ever, will have no memory of earth time. Yet, God saw it proper for Jesus and the angels to look upon the lake of fire forever. Point being, God has allowed man to know things of earth and some in heaven. However, this man's perception is, man can never know all of God. Does man need to know all of God? Would He still be God if man was equal to God? **Jesus does as He hears and sees God!** --- **His delight is in pleasing God!** ---(Deut.29:29 **the secret things belong to the Lord our God; but the things that are <u>revealed</u>**

belong to us and to our children for ever that we may do all the words of this law

So very many people want to know God's truth of prophecy, but know, what they have heard is most likely imagination. Not this man, nor can any other man teach God's truth! It only comes as truth from the Holy Spirit! The only thing one can do for another person is to point the direction of where the Spirit began with themselves. Each, must search the scriptures, daily, to know if what they heard is truth.

This man's speaking and writing is all about pointing out the direction to the Holy Spirit. Hopefully, with the Spirit's guidance, some people will have a good-enough foundation laid for the wise/ those that fear God, to come to truth and be prepared for the sour stomach that is coming.

Those that have had the revealing of the beast from the sea, know all things in God's teachings is connected from beginning to ending. All things that were created is good. It is man's reasoning, to take God's good and turn it into his own/bad. As the serpent decreed: if you go against God's command, then you have what is necessary to become a god. Had not God, already decreed man to have charge of all God's property? Therefore, it was a matter of which one man would accept (same is true today). For, God has given man a chance to change his mind and come back to God, through His Son/let there be light.

The serpent is making a counterfeit/his son of perdition/ with spirit of deception. God, then is willing to send His very Spirit to all, whom believed His Son/Light, that deception will have no power over us. God has proven this through the Jew and the Gentile. Now, the earth is only continuing for the sake of God's great name!

Final-Time-Line for Jews: Deuteronomy 18:18 **I will raise up for them a prophet like you** (Moses) **from among their brethren; and I will put My words in His mouth and He** (Jesus) **shall speak to them all that I command Him. Whoever will**

34

not **give heed** to **My words** which He shall speak in **My name, I Myself will require it of** **him**.

---FIRST the Jew, said it is all false. Then the Gentile said God got it wrong. (Between the banks of the river: Who can stand on water) ---Jesus told Gabriel to tell Daniel, **"consider** (meditate) **the** **word** **and understand the** **vision**". **Seventy weeks of years** (7x70=490years) **are decreed concerning your people** (Jew) **and** **your holy city** (Jerusalem) (REMEMBER: Jeremiah: 70 continual years of desolation/God has always given a small sample before the big happening)

To finish the transgression (not obedient to God) **to put an end to sin** (sin is lawlessness) (John 9:31 *we know God does not listen to sinners, but if anyone is a worshipper of God and does His will, God listens to him.*) --- **and to atone for iniquity** (Prov.16:6*By loyalty and faithfulness iniquity is atoned for*) (Eccl. 3:16 *moreover, I saw under the sun that in the place of justice, even there was wickedness and in the place of righteousness* (Noah & Abraham believed God and it was reckoned unto them for righteousness), *even there was wickedness. I said in my heart, God will judge the righteous and the wicked, for He has appointed a time for every matter and for every work. I said in my heart with regard to the sons of men that God is testing them to show them that they are* ***but beasts***) (Jesus said, God does not temp man.) Therefore, Solomon's word "testing" would mean, God is allowing man to run his own course.---**to bring in everlasting righteousness to seal both vision and prophet** (the same as the beginning; if the Jew would have chosen to believe God and follow His will, the end of this prophecy would not come to pass and the book of Daniel would be disregarded.) **know therefore and** **understand** that **from the going forth** of the **word** to **restore** and **build Jerusalem** to the coming of an **anointed one, a prince, there** **shall be** seven weeks (7x7=49years).This is where the hand-me-down-delusion begins and the whole world wonders after the beast and worships his image. God's image is truth-versus-the beast image is deception from the truth. (Remember the dude breaking the yoke off Jeremiah, the same has taken place by preachers with Gabriel's word)

Gentiles say God got it wrong on the time lines. Therefore, the best thing to do is take a week of years and throw it out into the future and dedicate the week to satan and claim the prophecy to be for sixty-nine weeks of years. Preacher/priest begin their delusional preaching with the first chapter of Ezra. What does it say? **"Rebuild the house of the Lord"**. What did Gabriel say? **"Restore and build Jerusalem"**. Jerusalem is not the house of the Lord!

"Seventh-day man-churches" got it a little closer, but still just delusion. For, they use Ezra 6:6-8---still talking about rebuilding of **this house of God.** They claim God is poor in math and man has to help Him get it right. **"And the whole world wondered after the beast and worshipped his image."**

The true "word" (did not say command), came in Nehemiah 2:5 *I said to the king, if it please the king and if your servant has found favor in your sight that you send me to Judah to the city of my father's sepulchers that I may rebuild it. The king said to me (the queen sitting beside him), how long will you be gone and when will you return? So it pleased the king to send me.*

Further proof of the delusion is, man-churches say the wall around Jerusalem took less than two months to build. This comes from Nehemiah 6:15. This man has tried to get preachers and deacons, (deacons being another delusional practice: Remember Phoebe) to look at chapter 5:14 *moreover, from the time that I was appointed to be their governor in the land of Judah, from the twentieth year to the thirty second year of Artaxerxes the king twelve years---V.16: I also held to the work on this wall* With Nehemiah working on the wall for twelve years, how could it possibly have been built in less than two months? The preachers told this man, "that stuff does not matter, just listen to what is being taught, for these men/ teachers are very spiritual". This kid had wondered after the beast long enough! There was only one thing for me to do: shake the dust off my feet as I was leaving. Some people have looked at the scripture, but **from fear of being put out of the church** by those that "supposedly" have a closer connection to God, will not turn to God. "Man is a <u>social animal</u>" not "a child of God"

REMEMBER: Gabriel said it would be forty-nine years after the <u>word</u> to restore and rebuild Jerusalem, before rebuilding of the city would begin. Building the wall began in the twentieth year of Artaxerxes. Neh.7:1-4 verse 4: *the city was wide and large, but the people within it were few and no houses had been built.* John 2:20 *the Jews then said, "It has taken <u>forty-six years</u> to build this temple."* (From Cyrus command until sixth year of Darius was fifty-eight years. Temple was finished before wall was finished.

Both old and new testimonies say to **not put your faith nor trust in a friend or guide. Daily, search the scripture to see if what is said, is truth!** Today, around the world, people are in a great hypnotic-trans from deception in God's word and there appears to be no way of recovery!

Jesus, even yelled "9-1-1" to the United States, through God parting the sea for a pickup load of goat herders, with plastic knives, to come and bring nationwide fear on the most powerful country on earth. They simply destroyed the temples of almighty-dollar.

Then God brought *"the seas upon dry land"* in the gulf-coast and on the eastern United States. Preachers were finally telling the truth, "We just do not know why God has allowed these things to happen."---It will be coming worse! The world would not be, today, but for God's longsuffering!

All today, is the same as when God was on the mountain talking to His people. His thundering and lightening will not be listen to. Therefore, this man is under no delusion that people might listen to what the Spirit has revealed to me. However, the Lord is compelling me to try.

Retuning to Gabriel, for there is much more diluted truth. **Then for sixty-two weeks (7x62=434 years) it shall be built again with squares and moat, but in a troubled time. After the sixty-two weeks (49+434=483 years), <u>an anointed one shall be cut off and shall have nothing</u>** Mark 1:2-3 *as it is written in Isaiah the prophet, "Behold, I send My messenger before thy face, who shall prepare thy way; the voice of one crying in the wilderness: prepare the way of the Lord, make His paths straight* ---**and the people** (Romans) **of the prince** (satan) **<u>who is to come</u> shall destroy the city and the sanctuary. Its end shall come with a flood and to the end there shall be war; desolations are decreed** (I have heard all the preacher sermons that it was a flood of blood down the temple steps or a flood of people leaving Israel. One thing for sure, there was war between Jews and Romans and the Jew disburse throughout the world.)

However, by this part of the prophecy, <u>which is last</u>, being placed in the middle of the prophecy, verse-hoppers take off on a wild-goose-chase in their imagination. **HE** (is the coming of a prince). It is why God had <u>Jerusalem</u> rebuilt (Deut.18).

The house of prayer was rebuilt mainly for the sake of delusion on all that had no love for God's truth. God only allowed the temple built the first time, because of David's great love for God. But the people claimed the temple as god.

HE/JESUS: shall make a strong covenant with many for one-week (7 years +483=490years, all time-lines are recorded in scripture) LUKE: **beginning the fifteenth year of Tiberius Caesar,** which was 27AD. **Jesus being about thirty years old.** ---Jesus began His ministry mid-year between the pass-over and it lasted three-and-one-half years.

<u>**And for half of the week**</u> He (Jesus) **shall cause sacrifice and offering to cease** (Remember: Jesus braded a wipe and run the retail-god-business out of the temple.) **upon the wing of abominations** (three and one half years after Jesus' death (34AD), Stephan recounted the entire teaching of God. He was stoned to

death for speaking the scripture.) Scripture says, man-church will again be killing multiples of God's people.

Matthew 27:25 *all the people* (mostly Jews) *answered, "His blood be on us and on our children!"* (We can see God granted their request for fourteen generations) Acts 18:5 *Paul was occupied with preaching, <u>testifying to the Jews</u> that <u>the Christ was Jesus</u>. When they opposed and reviled him, he shook out his garments and said to them, "your blood be upon your heads! I am innocent.* The stoning of Stephan (34AD) was the end of the seventy-week prophecy, to which the Jews would not accept God's terms! **shall come one who makes desolate, until the decreed end is poured out on the desolator."** As was with Job, God told satan to have at it with the Jews, but he cannot completely destroy them. Satan tried again to overrule God through the holocaust.

NOTE: why did Jesus choose Saul for the replaced twelfth apostle? Saul truly loved God; because of deception Saul thought Jesus to be just another occult, trying to attack his God! ---Same today, Jesus will go an extra mile for one that truly loves God.

Chapter 7

RUNNING THE COURSE: SATAN-V-JEW

"Shall come one who makes desolate, until the decreed end is poured out on the desolator." For the wise that the Spirit has given understanding thus far, deception/delusion has to this day been far greater than what was up to 34AD! It will get worse! Saying, **Peace, peace and there will be no peace!** Since probably 1948, we have entered the beginning of sorrows.

Many have believed themselves to be of the elect of God and will continue to believe it so. Hopefully, some will search the scripture to see if it truly is the Spirit that gave this little book. As was with this man, find that it was my imagination telling me that I was held blameless. **The seal of God, is this, God is true!** The new heaven and new earth will be eternal. The "new" will have to be of one-mind!

Could God bring judgment on the earth, when heaven was also dirty (defiant angels)? God had decreed the seventy weeks of years for His chosen people to get right with Him. Therefore, heaven had to be clean before the eternal priest could take office.

Daniel 10: **in the third year of Cyrus king of Persia a word was revealed to Daniel, who was named Belteshazzar. The word was true and it was a great conflict. <u>He understood the word and had understanding of the vision</u>.** The Lord did not go into detail, but for those with love for God's truth, <u>the Spirit!!!</u> Those without love for God: it makes the imagination run wild into more delusion.

When looking back before the great flood, angels whom left their proper place, were making children with the daughters of men and men had no control. The offspring were called "mighty men". After the great flood, Nimrod was called "the first of the mighty men". Some have claimed Samson to be angelic offspring. This man would not argue the point, but just say, nothing happens less it be within God's purpose. The Philistine giants were angelic offspring, as well as the one tribe in Benjamin that the entire Israeli army had great difficulty in defeating.

NOTE: all of them **were left-handed**

NOTE: one must **be born of <u>water</u> and of <u>spirit</u> before they can enter heaven.** If one were born from woman, they were born of water. Remember: originally even dust was created from a ball of water. Angel=spirit: improperly leaving heaven, cannot return. (Are we truly reborn in God's Spirit?)

This man has had many left-handed relatives; stands to reason there would be angelic back ground. However, with the Spirit revealing God's truth to me, says, I have been reborn in the Spirit. Praise be to God!

<u>Consider,</u> why will the mark of the beast be placed on the right-hand? Or why does Jesus set on the right-hand of God? Why did God tell Israel to kill every living thing in the kingdoms of Canaan, even live-stock? Good or bad, **all knowledge comes from God!** Improper angels taught man to fornicate with animals and with other men. On close study one will find this to be the reason God utterly destroyed **Sodom, Gomorrah and all the valley and all the inhabitants of the cities and what grew on the ground.** God has not ordered man to do anything He has not done Himself! Another proof of being an Almighty God!

Is the Spirit revealing how the great pyramids and other huge structures were built and why the majority of them are below the thirty-second degree north? God does not just ask us to believe Him. God said He left **"shades of things"** that we today, may know He has told the truth in the past.

Consider, why assassination of kings was never heard of until Jews had kings? A person that obeys God has no idea of how much God is protecting them. Also, because men such as this man has chosen to follow Jesus, other people have been protected: on returning to U.S. from the Nam, this man hated all people! When realizing I hated myself more, was when God could remold me!

We know war in heaven had not taken place by the time Jacob fought with the angel. For the angel could not mix with light. It did not happen in David's time, because David killed an angelic offspring. (David's thirty body-guards were angelic offspring: reborn into God's Spirit)

Daniel 10:2 **in those days I, Daniel, was mourning for three weeks. I ate no delicacies, no meat or wine entered my mouth, nor did I anoint myself at all for the full three weeks**. The chapter goes on to explain Jesus, Himself, came to give Daniel understanding of why it must be and to give him comfort.

Daniel 10:12 **then He** (Jesus) **said to me, fear not, Daniel, for from the first day that you set your mind to understand and humbled yourself before your God, your words have been heard and I have come because of your words** (Jesus still does the same today)

Verse 13: **the prince of the kingdom of Persia withstood Me twenty-one days** NOTE: God has made very clear (Daniel's vision), of being literal 21 days in man-time. The "prince" of the kingdom is the one that is always meddling in God's business. Daniel was already in the kingdom and Jesus came to Daniel. (Joshua: who is the commander of the Lord's army) **but Michael, one of the chief princes, came to help Me, so I left him there with the prince of the kingdom of Persia -**

NOTE: in the third year of Cyrus king of Persia, there was no war taking place in, nor, by the kingdom. This does not necessarily mean war was taking place in heaven, yet, it does not mean it was not. We must be for sure. **-and came to make you understand what is to befall your people** (Jews) **in the latter days. For the vision is for days yet to come**. Consider: God's time, 12+21=33years of man-life. When did Jesus begin His Father's business? Was David greater than Jesus? Solomon said, "What has been is what will be"

Verse 20: **but now I will return to fight against the prince of Persia; and when I am through with him** (was there any doubt), **Lo, the prince of Greece will come** (satan not destroyed). **But I will tell you what is inscribed in the book of truth: there is none who contends by My side against these except Michael, your** (Jews) **prince.** JUDE 9:*when the archangel Michael, contended with the devil, disputed about the body of Moses, he did not presume to pronounce a reviling judgment upon him, but said, "the Lord rebuke you"* Jesus nor Michael had authority to pass judgment, only to perform the will of God. NOTE: God allows understanding when we are able to absorb it.

Example: this man devoted five years to searching God's two witnesses. For I knew the hand-me-down religion out of preacher mouths was not right. When the Spirit finally revealed the truth of God's two witnesses, I thought, this is so easy, LORD, why did I not see it long ago? As more of God's truths came, I realized, from the Spirit, many other things had to be understood before I could handle this truth. Point being, God always answers prayer. Most of the time He says NO! When the time is right and the question is within God's will, He will grant it! It depends on us being a workman unto God. **God helps those that help themselves!** God is not a field-hand for anyone.

Revelation 12: (Sake of God's elect, anointed from heaven to bring forth a man child) **another portent appeared in heaven;**

behold, a great red dragon, with seven heads and ten horns, and seven diadems upon his heads. By the time Mary was in labor to deliver Jesus, God had preordained who and by what means satan would use to deceive the world. God had gave judgment on satan, but also gave a stay of execution. Satan was the tool God used to try the angels, the Jews and now he would try the gentiles.

Verse 7: **now war arose in heaven, Michael and his angels fighting against the dragon; and the dragon and his angels fought, but they were defeated and there was no longer any place for them in heaven. And the great dragon was thrown down, that ancient serpent, who is called the devil and satan, the <u>deceiver of the whole world</u> --- he was thrown down to the earth and his angels were thrown down with him** (other scripture tells us the fallen angels were chained away in the pit. It is man's own lust that is his demons.) **I heard a loud voice in heaven, saying, now the salvation and the power and the kingdom of our God and the authority of His Christ have come, for the accuser of our brethren has been thrown down, who accuses them day and night before our God. They have conquered him <u>by the blood of the Lamb</u> and <u>by the word of their testimony,</u>** (Not in a building of seclusion, with like-minded people, but in the highways& hedges) **for they loved not their lives even unto death. Rejoice then, O heaven and you that dwell therein! But woe to you, O earth and sea, for the devil has come down to you in great wrath, because he knows that <u>his time is short</u>!**

By seventy AD. The Jews, through the seventy week of year's prophecy, had told God, He would just have to get over His bad self. Therefore, God dissolved the Jew nation and scattered them throughout the world.

Remember: Jesus riding the <u>unbroken colt</u> into Jerusalem and the people giving praise and glory. The preacher wanted Jesus to make them be quite. When the Jew was salted through the earth, he could not help but to tell the people in his new world, all about his history---**the rocks were crying out**! Revelation 14:6 **then I saw another angel flying in mid-heaven, with an <u>eternal gospel</u> to proclaim to those who dwell on earth, <u>to every nation and tribe and tongue and people</u>; he said with a loud voice, "<u>Fear God and give Him glory</u>, for <u>the hour</u> of <u>His judgment has come</u>** (it has already passed; JOHN12:28 *Father, glorify thy name. Then a voice came from heaven, I have glorified it and I will glorify it again. The crowed standing by heard it and said that it had thundered. Others said an angel has spoken to Him. Jesus answered, this voice has come for your sake, not for mine. <u>Now is the judgment of this world</u>, now shall the ruler of this world* (Jesus) *be <u>cast out</u>* (by people's unbelief in God) *and I, when I am lifted up from the earth, will <u>draw all men</u> to Myself.* It is still by choice of the individual! Man refused Jesus as king and Lord of earth: when Jesus gave up His Spirit and earth became dark-night in the middle of the day, is when satan and his band were cast into the earth; never to return to heaven. **(Prince** (satan) **who is to come shall destroy the city and the sanctuary)**

Why did God prune the gentile and graft the Jew back into the stump? For, the Jew (70 weeks of year's prophecy) had denied God and followed the dragon; becoming the dragon! Gentile-Christen did no better: followed deception of satan; became the beast kingdom!

Chapter 8

RUNNING THE COURSE: SATAN-V-GENTILE

Revelations 12:13 **when the dragon saw that he had been thrown down to the earth, he pursued the woman** (all who fear God) **who had borne the male child. But the woman was given the two wings** (God's two witnesses) **of the great eagle that she might fly from** (deception) **the serpent into the wilderness** (living in the world but holding to God), **to the place where she is to be nourished** (Holy Spirit's revealing) **for a time and times and half a time**.

Revelation 11:2 **but do not measure the court outside the temple; leave that out, for it is given over to the nations and they will trample over the holy city for <u>forty two months</u> and I will grant <u>My two witnesses</u> power to prophesy for <u>one-thousand-two-hundred-sixty</u> days, clothed in sackcloth.** All three time-lines equal the same amount. Time=1, times=2, 1+2=3+½=3.½,

Forty-two months=3.½ years, (the Hebrew calendar was thirty-day months) one-thousand-two-hundred-sixty, divided by thirty=forty-two. OR, in God's prophetic terms, days=years, 42months=3.½ years,
1260days=1260years.

Ezekiel: **see I give you a day for each year.** Vatican City was established in Rome Italy 529AD. One-thousand-two-hundred-sixty years later 1789AD. Vatican-City-nation was abolished.

529 AD through 1789 AD, ---twelve-thousand from each of the twelve tribes of Israel (holding God's two witnesses) went throughout the earth proclaiming: **"Fear God and give Him glory, for the hour of His judgment has come; and worship Him who made heaven and earth, the sea and the fountains of water."**--- **"Go into the world teaching what so ever I have commanded you, baptizing in the name of the Father, Son, and Holy Spirit"**

Rev.14: **then I looked and Lo, on Mount Zion stood the Lamb and with Him a hundred and forty-four-thousand who had His name and His Father's name written on their foreheads, who had been redeemed from the earth.** (1789) **It is these who have not defiled themselves with women, for they are chaste; it is these who follow the Lamb wherever He goes; these have been redeemed from mankind as first fruits for God and the Lamb.** ---could it be said that the so-called secret-rapture has come and gone? Or is secret-rapture just more **pretend signs and wonders** for those that would rather believe a lie? What could be secret where it is for-told? **When they say I am in the secret chamber believe it not!** Jesus knew 2000yrs. before the false prophecy would come!

We know Jews were not pure blood, not even Jesus (Tamar &Ruth); no one on earth today can honestly say they are of Jew blood (Abraham, Isaac, Jacob), nor can anyone honestly say they are not. Matthew 13: **I will open My mouth in parables, I will utter what has been hidden since the foundation of the world.** John 1: **Jesus saw Nathanael coming to Him and said of him, Behold, an Israelite indeed, in whom is no guile!** (Jew nor Gentile has no bearing on this statement, Jesus is speaking about individual people)---**from these stones, God is able to raise up children to Abraham.**

After the resurrection of Jesus and the death of the twelve apostles, there have been no more prophets nor Apostles (men claim to be but, it was Jesus who appointed the replaced twelfth); it is in the scripture. However, Rev.19:10 **worship God. For the testimony of Jesus is the <u>spirit of prophecy</u>.** Everyone with a love for God's truth, have already or will soon have a revealing from the Spirit concerning this last teaching from Jesus' servant.

Rev.11:4 (is time from 1948 until the rise of the lawless one) **these are the two olive trees** (God-fearing Jew& Gentile) **and the two lamp stands** (God-fearing Jew &Gentile) **which stand before the Lord** (Jesus) **of the earth. ---And when they have finished their testimony, the beast that ascends from the bottomless pit** (1929) **will make war upon them** (deception and delusion so strong (man-church); if it were possible would even fool the very elect of God) **and conquer them and kill them and their dead bodies will lie in the street of the great city which is allegorically called Sodom and Egypt, where their Lord was crucified.** (When two-hundred-million-man-armies surround Jerusalem) **For three days and a half men from the peoples and tribes and tongues and nations gaze at their dead bodies and refuse to let them be placed in a tomb** (until they swell-up and stink that everyone will have no doubt that they are dead) **after the three and a half days a breath of life from God entered them and they stood up on their feet and great fear fell on those who saw them. Then they heard a loud voice from heaven saying to them, "Come up hither" and in the sight of their foes they went up to heaven in a cloud.**

NOTE: God told us, by the prophets, those remaining will bury bodies and gather the weapons for their fires for seven years after Armageddon. Jeremiah said these people (especially women) will revert back to man-church.

However, this is also the time that seven women will ask one man for his name (1/10th. World population left alive; 7to1 women). God is leaving no excuse! Nothing is coming that has not already been done on a small scale! It is all in the scripture; intelligence will not reveal it!

Building the beast: Daniel 7:7 **a fourth beast, terrible and dreadful and exceedingly strong; it had great iron teeth; it devoured and broke in pieces and stamped the residue with its feet. It was different from all the beasts that were before it; it had ten horns**. How could Rome be different from the other three world kingdoms? --- It still rules the world today and will rule until the appearing of the Lord! The Jew decreed it to be so, now the Gentile has decreed it to be so.

I considered the horns and behold, there came up among them another horn, a little one, before which three of the first horns were plucked up by the roots; behold, in this horn were eyes like the eyes of a man and a mouth speaking great things. As Solomon said, "men are beasts". From a small leadership, has come a world-wide beast that rules the hearts and minds of men. However, God still has a small remnant of people salted throughout the earth that are governed by their conscience and faith that the Lord is true.

Revelation 2:19 **I know your works, your love and faith and service and patient endurance and that your latter works exceed the first** (many people today, though they do not know truth of scripture, sense the end of time is near. These are beginning to at least come to some of the love Jesus portrayed for people and trying to draw strength from those that have a sense of enter peace) **but I have this against you, that you tolerate the woman Jezebel** (Vatican City/great harlot) **who calls herself a prophetess and is teaching and beguiling My servants to practice immorality** (denominational-man-church, away from

God's commands) **and to eat food** (false teaching) **sacrificed to idols. <u>I gave her time to repent</u>** (1789-1929) **but she refuses to repent of her immorality.**

Rev.4: after this I looked, and LO, in heaven an open door! The first voice, which I had heard speaking to me like a trumpet, said, come up hither and I will show you what <u>must take place after this</u> (did not say Jews), **at once I was in the Spirit** (flesh & blood cannot enter heaven) **and LO, a throne stood in heaven, with one seated on the throne! He who sat there appeared like jasper and carnelian and round the throne was a rainbow that looked like an emerald. Round the throne were twenty-four thrones, seated on the thrones <u>were twenty-four elders</u>**

We need to stop here and clear the mind of multiple delusions: Matthew 27:51 *and behold, the curtain of the temple was torn in two, from top to bottom; and the earth shook and the rocks were split; the tombs also were opened and many bodies of the <u>saints</u> who had fallen asleep were raised and coming out of the tombs <u>after</u> **His** (Jesus) <u>resurrection</u> they went into the holy city and appeared to many. --- It is appointed unto man once to die then the judgment* --- "Saints" says they were judged blameless and they did not die a second death. But, have they been seen lately (24-Elders)

NOTE: Saints were long before popes & Vatican City

Rev.5: I saw in the <u>right-hand</u> of Him who was seated on the throne a scroll written within and on the back, <u>sealed with seven seals</u>; I saw a strong angel proclaiming with a loud voice, "who is worthy to open the scroll and break its seals?" --- Then one of the elders said to me, "weep not; Lo, the Lion of the tribe of Judah, the Root of David, has conquered, so that He can open the scroll and its seven seals." Between the throne and the four living creatures and among the elders, I saw a

Lamb standing as though it had been slain, with seven horns and with seven eyes, which are the seven spirits of God <u>sent out into all the earth</u>; He went and took the scroll from the <u>right-hand</u> of Him who was seated on the throne.

Rev. 6: **When the Lamb (Jesus) opened one of the seven seals I heard one of the four living creatures say "Come", I saw, and behold, a white horse** ("white" is representation of God's will---"horse" is representation of power), **its rider had a bow** (represents strife and war); **a crown was given to him** (God's purpose), **and he** (Napoleon) **went out conquering and to conquer** (all seven western European heads and dissolve papal Rome)

He opened the second seal. I heard the second living creature say, "Come", out came another horse, bright red (representing spilled blood); **its rider was permitted to take peace from the earth, so that men should slay one another; and he was given a great sword.** --- It was called, "World War One"

When He opened the third seal, I heard the third living creature say, "Come", and I saw, and behold, a black horse (represents evil), (1929: United States breathed life back into the beast from the sea Rev.9: *the fifth angel blew his trumpet and I saw a star fallen from heaven to earth, he was given the key of the shaft of the bottomless pit; he opened the shaft of the bottomless pit and from the shaft rose smoke like the smoke of a great furnace and the sun and the air were darkened with the smoke from the shaft.*) There are still today, living witnesses of "Dust bowl days" **and its rider had a balance in his hand** Daniel: 5 *God, in whose hand is your breath and whose are all your ways, you have not honored. Then from His presence, the hand was sent and this writing was inscribed Mene, Mene, Tekel and Parsin. Mene/God has numbered the days of your kingdom and brought it to an end* (United States); *Tekel, you have been* <u>*weighed in the balances and found wanting*</u>*; Peres, your kingdom is divided and given to the Meds and Persians* (literally the U. S... True combat veterans have no problem seeing this because, American-government is so predictable in greed: foundation of the nation is rapidly being eroded away. Veterans are considered radical-delusional); **and I heard what seemed to be a voice in the midst of the four living creatures saying, "A quart of wheat for a denarius and three quarts of barley for a denarius; but do not harm oil and wine** (wheat& barley represent shortage of food and money to buy. Oil & wine represent anointed/salvation & teaching from God) Has the revealing come of "not buy or sell without the mark of the beast"? Both old and new testimonies say, **"For those who love the Lord, they shall eat of the fruit of their doing"**

When He opened the fourth seal, I heard the voice of the fourth living creature say "Come" and I saw and, behold, a pale horse (represents God allowing satan, that God's purposes be fulfilled), **and its rider's name was Death and Hades followed him; and they were given power over a fourth of the EARTH, to KILL with SWORD and with FAMINE and with PESTILENCE and by WILD BEASTS of the EARTH.** --- It was called World War II. ---A combat solder can see the value of a God made of love. Even the supreme allied commander of WW II, though not a combat solder, on becoming President of the U.S. decreed the United States to be, "One Nation under God." At that time, eighty-nine percent of those professing a god, was the **God of Abraham, Isaac, and Jacob.** None denied the decree and for as many as have died for this decree, it cannot be voted out, only a civil war can change it: now in process through religious & civil liberties. God said civil will win.

History tells us, the U.S. entered WWI because of business investments in Europe. Again WW II American business investments. However, the general public still remembered the first war and knowing who would have to die and who would stay safe, the majority were reluctant to enter. The national organization of so-called "Christen men" devised a plan of reneging on a business deal with Japan and setting bait to draw them in, which changed public opinion.

NOTE: Japan was not considered to be Europe, but shortly after Pearl Harbor armies were sent to Europe. Leaving the East coast open for attack by German U-boats!

NOTE: every war America has entered since WW II the same tactic has been used to get public approval, with the exception of President concocting the WMD project, to which still brought fear on the public. Over all, a great victory for false prophet.

Micah 7:3 *their <u>hands</u> are upon what is evil, to do it diligently; the prince and the judge ask for a bribe, and the great man utters the evil desire of his soul; thus they weave it together. The best of them is like a brier, the most upright of them a thorn hedge.*

When He opened the fifth seal, I saw under the alter the souls of those who had been slain for the word of God and for the witness they had borne; they cried out with a loud voice, "O Sovereign Lord, holy and true, how long before thou wilt judge and avenge our blood on those who dwell upon the earth?" Then they were each given a white robe and told to rest a little longer, <u>until the number of their fellow servants</u> (saints/blameless) and <u>their brethren</u> (one flock) should be complete <u>who were to be killed</u> as <u>they themselves had been.</u> The revealing of the Holocaust!

THIS is the POINT in TIME of the WORLD today! ---Between the opening of the fifth and sixth seal!

Chapter 9

SIXTH SEAL

Amazing, the number of preachers this man has heard say, they will be glad to see The Day of the Lord come. They preach it as another day of Pentecost (Joel's prophecy of when people will again prophesy God's will) The Day of the Lord/Jesus' second coming/opening of the sixth seal, is the most spoken of subject in scripture. Yet, very, very few people have understanding.

Amos 5:18 *Woe to you who desire the day of the Lord! Why would you have the day of the Lord? It is darkness, and not light; as if a man fled from a lion, and a bear met him; or went into the house and leaned with his hand against the wall and a serpent bit him. Is not the day of the Lord darkness and not light and gloom with no brightness in it?* --- REV.14:13 *blessed are the dead <u>who die in the Lord</u> henceforth. "Blessed indeed," says the Spirit, "that they may rest from their labors, for their deeds follow them!"*

Rise of the lawless one: the number of the last to hold "God's two witnesses" (God's remnant), we cannot know. This man perceives it maybe as Abraham pleaded for his family in Sodom. Rev.11:11**but after the three and a half days a breath of life from God entered them and they stood up on their feet and great fear fell on <u>those who saw them.</u> Then they heard a loud voice from heaven saying to them, "Come up hither!"---and <u>the rest</u> were terrified and gave glory to the God of heaven.**

AMOS 8:11 *behold, the days are coming, says the Lord God, when I will send a famine on the land; not a famine of bread, nor a thirst for water, but of hearing the words of the Lord. They shall wander from sea to sea, and from north to east; they shall* *run to and fro, to seek the word of the Lord, but they shall **not** find it.* ---The Lord is talking about the time God's Spirit no longer dwells with man (when the two witnesses rise to God). However, **those terrified and gave glory to the God of heaven---** *All who call upon the name of the Lord* (God has given one name by which man) *shall be saved!* ---1 Corinthians15:51**LO! I tell you a mystery. We shall not all sleep, but we shall all <u>be changed</u>, in a moment, in the <u>twinkling of an eye</u>, at the <u>last trumpet</u>.** (No one should be trying to catch this bus for it will be those that give praise to God and cry out to Jesus when they see the two witnesses rise to Jesus. Do it before hand) **For the trumpet will sound and the dead will be raised imperishable and we shall be changed. For this perishable nature must put on the imperishable and this mortal nature must put on immortality. When the perishable puts on the imperishable and the mortal puts on immortality, then shall come to pass the saying that is written: "Death is swallowed up in victory."**

Rev.20:4 *then I saw thrones and seated on them were <u>those to whom</u> judgment was committed. <u>Also</u> I saw the souls of those who had been beheaded for their testimony to Jesus and for the word of God and who had not worshipped the beast or its image and had not received its mark on their foreheads or their hands* (All have! But, in Jesus' name, God has wiped it from His mind). *<u>They came to life</u> and <u>reigned with Christ a thousand years</u>. The <u>rest of the dead did not come to life</u> until the thousand years were ended, this is the first resurrection. Blessed and holy is he <u>who shares in the first resurrection</u>! Over such the second death has no power. Clad in white garments, with golden crowns upon their heads.* Jesus has the authority to forgive all sins, but one, and He is the <u>ONLY ONE</u> that has achieved this height, ---but time is very short! Have popes& priest proved their authority to forgive as did Jesus?

For the fact that after people may have read to this point and there will be many scoffers, I am compelled to go further!

Revelation 13:11 **Then I saw another beast which rose out of the earth** remember 1789AD. The leader of the beast from the sea received a wound unto death. The world was given time to repent (140yrs. Or 7 times) for following false teaching (satan has a short time and is determined to take as many as possible with him; it is his only way of hurting God) **"out of the earth"** means they were already a recognized people (seven western European nations) that came together and formed another nation/kingdom. This kingdom would have to be established before 1929. But after 1789. The adopting of the Constitution of the United States 1798. It was put together with two governing factors **it had two horns like a lamb and it spoke like a dragon.**

It exercises all the authority (the first two presidents of twenty-first century had other world leaders assassinated) **of the first beast in its presence and makes the earth and its inhabitants worship the first beast,** (presidents chumming with popes and the nation not standing against it, say, the U.S. has culled God) **whose mortal wound was healed. It works great signs, even making fire come down from heaven** (onto Hiroshima Japan) **in the sight of men; and by the signs which it is allowed to work in the presence of the beast it deceives those who dwell on earth** (each new president, visits the pope to discuss world matters: mystery Babylon; leader in world stock exchange), **bidding them make an image** (it is good politics to say one is Christen; they all have the same format!) **for the beast which was wounded by the sword** (God's Spirit) **and yet lived; it was allowed to give breath to the image of the beast** (Mussolini wanted to build Rome to its former glory with himself as Caesar. U.S. changed his mind and restored papal Rome) **so that the image of the beast should even speak** (U.S. decreed man-church, the word of god) **and to cause those who would not worship the image of the beast to be slain** (when Virginia encompassed most of the east coast, they had a law that anyone missing three Sunday-go-to-meetings would be killed) **also it causes All, both**

small and great, both rich and poor, both free and slave, to be marked on the <u>right hand</u> or the <u>forehead</u>, (the marks are placed by an angel and read by another angel) **so that no one can buy or sell** (Mystery Babylon will control all food) **unless he has the mark, that is, the name of the beast** (Christen) **or the number of its name.** This set-up before the lawless one arrives

Note: check out the name under <u>The Vicar of Rome</u> (Corpus Juri Canonic) "<u>Vicarious Filii Dei</u>" Roman numerals total= 666

---"**Ten horns**" ---the three uprooted kingdoms, of the ten toes on the great image, will be replaced by the end of days. Remember, they must all be connected to the first four beast of Nebuchadnezzar's dream.

---The United States was initially formed from the seven western European kingdoms.

---It was pressure put on by the U.S. that reinstated Vatican City and the office of the son of perdition. Eighth=529 Vatican City, Ninth=622 false prophet, Tenth=1798 United States:

---**Ten toes**---

The United States was Jesus' last stand on earth. When presidents no longer **avoided them, in opposition to the doctrine we have been taught** and the people did not protest it, we were no longer a free nation/one nation under God, but an Ecclesiastical state/biggest hog at the trough. Now, for sure, the whole world wonders after the beast and worships his image! Will Jesus not soon be taking God's remnant out of the earth?

Is Jesus true? Deuteronomy 18:21-22 **when a prophet speaks in the name of the Lord, if the word does not come to pass or come true, that is a word which the Lord has not spoken; the prophet has spoken it presumptuously, you need not be afraid of him. (The revelation of Jesus Christ, which God gave Him to show to His servants what must soon take place; and He**

made it known by sending His angel to His servant John, who bore witness to the word of God and to the testimony of Jesus Christ.) Again, with so much of Jesus' prophecy fulfilled, <u>**is Jesus true?**</u>

Chapter 10

JESUS SAYING AWAKE

One must understand there are twelve prophecy points whereby to know who will be the son of perdition. There is only <u>one man</u> in <u>one position</u> that all points will line up. <u>He is not here yet</u>, but all has been placed for his arrival!

All popes to this point have "claimed" themselves to be Peter (Peter was a Jew: has there ever been a Jew pope) (with **Jesus healing his mother-in-law**, indicates Peter had desire of women), with power of Jesus to forgive sin (**all men have sinned and come short of the glory of God**). It will be the one that claims to be god above all known gods. **Even the God women love.** Women &children always flocked to Jesus!

A person with desire to be with the Lord, must wipe all delusion, preaching, teaching from the mind, <u>humble themselves before God</u> and <u>set their mind</u> to receive truth from God/believe all the scripture, <u>from Jesus approved scripture</u>! Both old and new testimonies say **those who are taught by God** (Holy Spirit revealing truth) **needs no other teacher.** It is called **"renewing the mind"**

Though the Spirit teaches <u>things yet to come</u>, this man will not go much further into it, for each must do their own relationship with Jesus! The scoffers would not believe if someone told them. All that matters is those that will come and that God's word be fulfilled. I will point out more of the false prophecy that comes from delusion.

It would be almost impossible to know truth by studying from other than Jesus approved scripture. Daniel chapter eight is talking about when the final pope takes office (the lawless one/doesn't keep any of God's law). Jesus was standing on the Ulai River, for who can walk on water? He called to Gabrie to make Daniel understand. **"He said to me, understand, O son of man that the vision** (ram& goat) **is for the time of the end".** --- **"Behold, a ram** (United States) **standing on the bank of the river** (water is people/the entire world). **It had two horns; and both horns were high, but one was higher than the other and the higher one came up last** (civil liberty; is it not evident today, with so much diarrhea coming out of the mouth of empty heads that have not paid for the country)

Behold, a he-goat came from the west across the face of the whole earth, without touching the ground (who was cursed from the ground? *Transgression of Adam, who was a type of the one who was to come--- he was a murderer from the beginning)*; **and the goat had a conspicuous horn** (beast kingdom leader) **between his eyes. The great horn of the goat was broken** (late seventeen-hundreds, the U.S. was a world factor in the industrial-age and had more natural resources than any other country. Vatican City was stock-exchange of the world (are we not supposed to labor with our hands). When V.C. was abolished, the world had problems adjusting, but by the early nineteen-hundreds, industry and stock markets were booming. When the U.S. brought V.C. back to life, the bottom fell out of the world and only world-evil/WW II could revive it; so people thought. **-and instead of it there came up four conspicuous horns** (kings) **toward the four winds** (strife& war) **of heaven** (Churchill, Roosevelt, Mussolini, Stalin summit). **-out of one of them came forth a little horn** (kingdom) **which grew exceedingly great toward the south, toward the east and toward the glorious land. It grew great, even to the host of heaven; and some of the host of the stars** (angels) **it cast down to the ground** (pope supposedly has power to excommunicate angels from heaven). **It magnified itself, even up to the Prince of the host** (Jesus, for, supposedly pope is god on earth); **and the continual burnt offering** (Spirit revealing) **was**

taken away from him and the place of his sanctuary (Vatican City) **was overthrown** (yet coming). **The host was given over to it** (control of all people, by choice of people) **together with the continual burnt offering through transgression** (one who understands riddles).

Already glaciers are melting fast and mountain snow is decreasing (main source of earth's fresh water). However, Israel's number one resource has always been underground water. It will be the world's only source of food. God said He **would put a hook in the mouth and draw them down.**

God works in mysterious ways! Satan tried the Jew in the same fashion as he did Job. However, the trying of the Gentile is amazing. Satan has done none other than to let God's blessing continue to flow on the ten horns of the beast kingdom. Continue, till gentile simply cannot get enough (I presume, power and status through wealth is a worse addiction than boos, dope or tobacco: it certainly causes more destruction). Same as the old Roman Empire.

Many people have more than they could spend in ten life times but, it is not enough. God said gold and silver will rust. Time is coming where people with a morsel of food will fight to the death to keep it (brother will turn sword on brother). Think not? God has already shown it when Jerusalem was besieged; women were eating their children. **Less God shorten the days there would be no flesh left. ---Their dead bodies shall be food for the birds of the air and the beasts of the earth.**

NOTE: there has always been multiples of delusion about the kingdom of the north. God calls Israel the center of the world and Jerusalem is its center (it is in the scripture). Jerusalem sets on the thirty-second degree north, same as Dallas Texas. (Have you heard the term thirty-second degree before): everything north of Jerusalem is the northern kingdom! All southern nations hold allegiance to one of the northern nations.

God's army will rise from the desert of Egypt and march through weapons of two-hundred-million man-world-army (<u>Not</u> one world government: son of perdition as allied commander!) --- and sweep across Israel from the brook of Egypt to Hamath, destroying everything in its path.

Evidently, the largest man-army ever assembled on earth, will be using weapons <u>like</u> flame-throwers and in-cinerary grenades. Because, in front of them, Israel will look like the Garden of Eden and behind them all will be ashes. Yet none of God's army will be stopped. It is all in the scripture!

It would be amazing to this man that the great army of man is going to destroy what they are <u>supposedly</u> going to be trying to save, but for being a war veteran, I know how politically lead armies think. It is not to save anything but, to have chaos that corporations that elected the officials may be justified in stealing from the presumed enemy. In this case the question will be asked, "Have you come for a spoil". **God is able and will abase.** ---**"Those that love the Lord shall eat of the fruit of their doing."**

Though this man has been given word from the Spirit to repeat to all others, people of the world will not heed to it. This I know because, God's word will be fulfilled!

Philippians 1:29 **for it has been granted to you that for the sake of Christ you should <u>not only believe</u> in Him <u>but also suffer</u> for His sake.**--- *"These are they who have come <u>out of the great tribulation</u>; they have washed their robes and made them white in the <u>blood of the Lamb</u>."* (Do you still believe garbage like "secret rapture"?) ---At this time the Spirit of God will no longer be dwelling with man, but as was Peter sinking in the sea and Said, "Lord save me" and Jesus pulled him up (**not all will sleep**).

Then I heard a holy one speaking and another holy one said to the one that spoke, "For how long is the vision concerning the <u>continual burnt offering</u> (Jesus' saving grace), the <u>transgression that makes desolate</u> and the <u>giving over</u> of the **<u>sanctuary</u>** (Holy Spirit no longer dwelling in man) **and <u>host</u> to be trampled under foot?**" Simply put, this is talking about the lawless one setting up his palatal tents at the gate of Samaria and ARMIES will be SURROUNDING Jerusalem.

NOTE: <u>No scripture</u> tracts to the valley of Megiddo. Simply imagination derived from one word. The battle will be throughout Israel with the main concentration in and around Jerusalem. **Of all the families of earth you are the one I have known. Therefore, I will punish you first.**

"**For two thousand and three hundred <u>evenings and mornings</u>** (literal days in man-time: 2300 days divided by 30=76.666 divided by 12 =6yrs and 39 days) However, during Jesus' ministry on earth, He said ***but for the <u>sake of the elect</u>, <u>whom He</u>*** (God) ***<u>Chose</u>*** (elect: God knows who will call on Jesus), ***He shortened the days.*** ---then the **<u>sanctuary</u>** (Holy Spirit again living in people) **shall be restored to its rightful state.**" (The beginning of the thousand years with Jesus) (So we still cannot know when "The Day of the Lord" is. But, we can know when it is close.)

After the world destroys the lawless-one& mystery Babylon and there is a short time before the day of the Lord, people still alive will revert back to man-church; it is recorded in Jeremiah. <u>NO one</u> will have cause to blame God!

It is recorded; at the opening of the sixth seal, Jesus holding up His hands and saying **all should be finished, but that the words of God be fulfilled:** The earth would continue for the full days of God's will. After the opening of the sixth seal, the prophets recorded, we will walk upon their ashes for one thousand years (Remember: the four in the fiery furnace. Remember: Math.3:11 He will baptize you with the Holy Spirit and with fire) literally! God has always given a small sample before the big one!

At the end of one thousand years satan will come alive from his first death. Where does satan get his army? For, son of perdition, fallen angels, beast and false prophet were cast into the lake of fire (whole world burning from meteor storm) at the opening of sixth seal. All blameless will be as the four in fiery furnace!

---Remember second death? Look to Ezekiel, the valley of dry bones/and ashes. **The rest of the dead did not come to life until the thousand years were ended.** Can earth hold that many people? The temple-mound will be the only mount on earth and there will be no more seas. Because, the opening of sixth seal will be with so severe Earth-quake that the earth will go out of orbit and no more mountains or valleys (Old Testament)

With the Holy Spirit giving this revealing from God, why should we gentiles help to rebuild Israel? Foremost, **the Lord said to!** Second, in the end Israel will be the only power left to stand against the son of perdition and his army/false prophet, Christen and atheist. Israel will be near to total annihilation when the nations of the world will destroy son of perdition and Vatican City.

But, how will the majority whom read this writing absorb it? Spirit of God to Micaiah: I Kings 22:8, **and the king of Israel said to Jehoshaphat, "there is yet one man by whom we may inquire of the Lord, Micaiah the son of Imlah; but I hate him** (same as was last to hold God's two witnesses)**, for he never prophesies good concerning me, but evil"**---verse 14, but Micaiah said, **"as the Lord lives, what the Lord says to me, that I will speak."** ---verse 18, and **the king of Israel said to Jehoshaphat, "did I not tell you that he would not prophesy good concerning me, but evil?"**

For the most part, people of today, are the same as was the king of Israel and the king of Judah. If one comes speaking God's truth and it does not conform to their desirers, they will proceed as did Balaam.

Verse 19, **"therefore hear the word of the Lord: I saw the Lord sitting on His throne and all the host of heaven standing**

beside Him on His right hand and on his left; and the Lord said, Who will entice Ahab, that he may go up and fall at Ramoth-gilead (dragon/Israel, beast kingdom/Christen and false prophet/Moslem are demonic spirits going to all the world enticing for the great battle of God?), **---a spirit said, I will entice him---I will go forth and will be a lying spirit in the mouth of all his prophets** (Priest/preachers/politician same as silver-smiths loosing trade.)

Spirit of God to Peter: II Peter 3:15 **count the forbearance of our Lord as salvation** (as long as we are alive we have opportunity for salvation). **So also our beloved brother Paul wrote to you according to the wisdom given him, speaking of this as he does in all his letters. There are some things in them hard to understand, which the ignorant and unstable/**pope, preacher, priest **twist to their own destruction, as they do the other scriptures. You therefore, beloved, knowing this beforehand, beware lest you be carried away with the error of lawless men** (has God's law truly been changed or done away with) **and lose your own stability. But grow in the grace and knowledge of our Lord and Savior JESUS CHRIST.**

Consider: In Noah's day God gave one-hundred-twenty years,
- --- God gave Jacob four-hundred years,
- --- God gave Judea seventy years,
- --- God gave the Jew nation four-hundred-ninety years,
- --- then, afterwards, God gave the Jews an additional thirty-six years before disbursing them,
- --- God gave the beast kingdom one-hundred-forty years to repent.

To this date of writing, God has given the United States eighty-five years to repent!

--- Sixty-six years since the Gentile was pruned from the cultivated stump!

--- how much longer can possibly be God's longsuffering?

The new Jew State, of 1948, has already received this word, but refuses it. No doubt in this man's mind that the United States and most all other Gentiles will refuse it. Because, Jesus said (as statement of fact), **"Many will knock but few will enter"** However, this man is only a watchman on the wall.

Job32:8 **but it is the spirit in a man, the breath of the Almighty that makes him understand.** ---to receive understanding from God is very sweet in the mouth. But, knowing how disobedient we have been is very bitter in the stomach.

THE END,
OR, THE BEGINNING